D0542156

Planting for Pleasure

By the same author

Creative Flower Arrangement
The Garden Indoors (with William Davidson)

Planting for Pleasure

Gardening and
Flower Arrangement

Jean Taylor

Stanley Paul,
London

Stanley Paul & Co. Ltd
3 Fitzroy Square, London W1

An Imprint of The Hutchinson Group

London Melbourne Sydney Auckland
Wellington Johannesburg Cape Town
and agencies throughout the world

First published 1973
© Thames Television Ltd 1973
Drawings © Stanley Paul & Co. Ltd 1973

Phototypeset in Monophoto Apollo
by Oliver Burridge Filmsetting Limited, Crawley
Made and printed in Great Britain

ISBN (C) 0 09 118300 6
       (P) 0 09 118301 4

Contents

Foreword   7

1 Arranging Cut Flowers   11
2 Roses   31
3 Spring Bulbs   57
4 Hardy Perennials   82
5 Shrubs   105
6 Dahlias   123
7 Flowers from Seed   142

Glossary   160
Addresses   165

'Whoever loves Nature will be loved by her in return and she will reveal secrets to him that he may create new things' Richard Zimmerman

Foreword

It has been said that Britain is a nation of gardeners. It is rapidly growing into a nation of flower arrangers also. Gardening has been the most popular outdoor interest for many years – chiefly because our climate lacks extremes and is conducive to the growth of such a great variety of plants with relative ease. Flower arranging looks as though it will become equally popular as an indoor interest. It is something with universal appeal – a practical visual art which does not require any elaborate skills or innate talent and which satisfies the need of the average person for creative self-expression. No art has spread with such rapidity or given as much active pleasure during the past twenty-five years. It has many facets: growing plants of special use for cutting; learning about basic design; collecting and making containers, bases and accessories for use with flowers; searching for driftwood and unusual materials; learning more about the natural world and developing a seeing eye; delving into unexpected subjects and places in the search for things; making friends through a similar interest. Moreover, in a world often fraught with tension and stress, such creative and satisfying activities as gardening and flower arranging give infinite peace.

The science of gardening and the art of flower arrangement have a great affinity. Both are deeply concerned with the beauty of the natural world, and it is no wonder that gardeners and flower arrangers are often happy companions. Many a flower arranger has turned gardener in order to broaden the scope of arranging flowers; and there can be few gardeners who have never arranged a cut flower, admired a design, or been without a secret wish to attempt one.

It is certainly possible to do one without the other. Flower arrangers can become accomplished if they use only shop flowers. Gardeners may gain enough satisfaction from seeing flowers in the garden without a need to see them in the home. But where

7

both thrive contentedly together there is greater satisfaction and happiness in an alliance which is creative and which beautifies both home and garden. The gardener and the flower arranger are often one and the same person, and at other times the occupations are shared and this gives a delightful family relationship. Apart from the love of living and beautiful plants what is the common ground? Basic design is a concern of the flower arranger but also of the gardener in planning a garden; colour organization and the need for textural contrasts and variety in shapes and patterns are of interest to both. The gardener who learns flower arrangement will find planning a garden comes more easily, that awareness of colours, shapes and textures will appreciate and consequently the combining of plants in the garden will become more exciting. The flower arranger who is also a gardener will create designs with greater interest if plants can be grown especially for cutting, and will see that there is colour in the garden all the year round for use in arrangements. Many flowers which can be used in the home never reach the shops and so in growing plants there is more scope for exciting colour schemes, contrasts of texture and variety of shape. It is also easier to pop into the garden to cut flowers and as a result they are arranged more frequently in the home and take less time and money. Best of all the garden and home can appear attractively related and each can be an extension of the other.

Acknowledgements

The author is very grateful to the Director and staff of the Royal Horticultural Society's garden, Wisley, Surrey, and to the Royal National Rose Society, St Albans, Hertfordshire for their invaluable assistance.

Copyright for the photographs is owned by the following: Pat Brindley, Robert J. Corbin, Douglas Rendell, Thames Television.

1 Arranging Cut Flowers

Flower arrangement can be an absorbing lifetime's study, but flowers may also be successfully arranged without knowing many of the finer points or spending a lot of time or money. It is necessary to know how to keep water flowing up the stem of the cut flower and how to hold the plant material in position in a container and then a start can be made. A minimum of equipment is necessary at first:

A pair of flower scissors. These are sold by garden centres, flower clubs and florists. They are better than domestic scissors as they cut stems cleanly.
One bucket. This is used for collecting cut flowers in the garden and for soaking stems in water. The type with a handle at each side is preferable as a central handle may crush flower heads.
A 3″ or 3½″ pinholder. This should have a heavy base and close, long pins.
Plasticine or a packet of Bostick No. 5

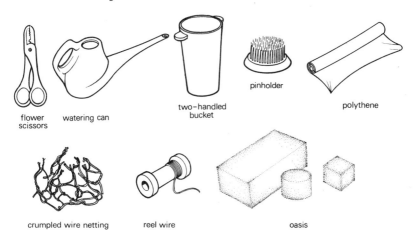

flower scissors   watering can   two-handled bucket   pinholder   polythene

crumpled wire netting   reel wire   oasis

11

A small watering can. A long spouted one is preferable.

Wire netting. 1 yard each of 1″ and 2″ mesh from an ironmonger.

A reel of florist's wire

Two broad rubber bands

Plastic foam. This is sold in blocks of varying size at florists. It is sold under several trade names, one of which is Oasis.

A sheet of polythene. This protects furniture and is useful for collecting rubbish.

Containers. Suggestions are:

1 A plastic saucer made to hold a block of Oasis and sold at florists or a small pottery bowl of about 5″ diameter;

2 A food tin painted with dark emulsion paint and deep enough to hold the pinholder and water to cover it;

3 A 12″ oval baking dish in an earthy colour such as brown, grey, dull green *or* a plant saucer of wide diameter which may be painted with emulsion paint in a similar colour;

4 A taller container, preferably bowl-shaped with a stem, in dull pottery, *or* a plant saucer glued to an upturned plant pot both made of plastic and painted in a dark, matt colour;

These four containers will give a variety of effects. Another useful possession is a base which could be:

1 A piece of slate or stone in an interesting shape;

A black-painted food tin, containing a pinholder, on a table mat

A plastic saucer holding Oasis, on a slip-covered cakeboard

Three useful containers and a wooden base

2 A crosscut of wood from a treetrunk;
3 A round tray about 12″ in diameter which can be 'slip-covered' with fabrics to give a variety of textures and colours. The base can be used under any of the containers. Other containers and bases can be added later.

The Need for Water

The stems of living flowers and leaves cut from a plant must stand in water otherwise they become limp and eventually wither and die.

WHEN CUTTING IN THE GARDEN

With the exception of the stems of Spring bulbous plants, it is better if the cut ends are placed in water immediately after cutting from the plant. This means taking a bucket half-full of water into the garden at cutting time and placing the stems into it at once. If this is not done air goes into the stem end and may form a bubble which prevents the uptake of water. It is better, in hot weather to cut when the plant contains more water – in the early morning.

Stem ends left out of water for some time often form a hard callus over the cut which also prevents the uptake of water. If a bucket cannot be taken into the garden the stem ends should be recut, removing about an inch of stem immediately before the flowers are placed in a bucket of water. This should cut off any air bubble or callus.

BEFORE ARRANGING

Some stem ends do not easily take up water and need to be encouraged with a little preparation. This should be done after cutting from the plant but before arranging, according to the stem type:

soft stems, such as annuals – no special treatment.

hard stems, such as roses – make a cut for about an inch up the stem to expose the inner tissue as this takes up water more readily than the harder outside.

woody stems, such as lilacs – scrape off the outside bark for 2" all around the base of the stem and cut up the stem for about 2". Water can then enter the stem more easily than it can through the hard bark.

milky stems, such as poppies – burn the stem end in a match or gas flame until it no longer sizzles. This stops the leakage but should be done again each time the stem is cut.

hollow stems, such as dahlias – upturn the stem and fill it with water using a funnel. Plug the stem end with cotton wool. This should be done each time the stem is cut.

Grooming

When plant material is picked it may have leaves which are damaged, diseased or eaten by insects. These should be removed as are unsightly. Dead or fading leaves and flowers should also be removed. Dirty foliage can be washed by swishing it around in a sink of water containing some detergent.

Leaves near the stem-end which would be under water in the arrangement should be removed as these decay and make the water slimy. *All stems,* with the exception of those growing from

14

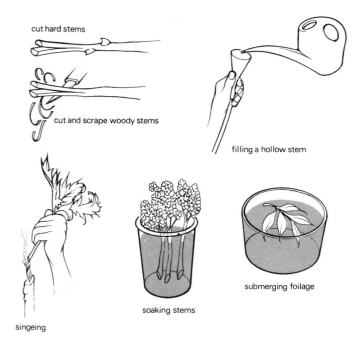

cut hard stems

cut and scrape woody stems

filling a hollow stem

singeing

soaking stems

submerging foilage

bulbs, which can become too soggy, then benefit from being soaked as deeply as possible in a bucket of warm water (at first) for two hours. This should be placed in a cool, dim place to cut down transpiration while the stems are being filled. The outside tissues of a stem as well as the stem end can also take in some water. Thorough soaking of the whole cutting is encouraged to absorb a maximum amount of water before being exposed to a dry, warm room where it may lose water rapidly.

Leaves can be well filled with water by submerging them in a sink of tepid water for about two hours which prevents transpiration. Water also enters through the tissue of the leaf as well as the stem end. Grey foliage should not be submerged or the greyness is lost.

IN AN ARRANGEMENT

The more flowers used in a design, the more water should be supplied for them and large arrangements need a big, container to hold plenty of water. This should never be allowed to dry out in any arrangement and water should be added every day or two by means of a watering can. This is called 'topping-up'. Occasionally flowers do wilt despite good stem-preparation or 'conditioning' as it is called. If this happens the limp flower should be removed and revived by the methods described in the following chapters for each type of flower.

THE PROVISION OF WATER

Water can be provided in two ways:

1 directly in the container;
2 by means of water retaining plastic foam (Oasis and others) into which stems are pushed.

Both are equally good but soft and hollow stems do not go into Oasis easily, and it is more expensive than using direct water. The advantage of Oasis is that it provides good support for many flower stems holding them exactly in position in addition to containing water. Oasis can dry out in a warm room and once it has done this it will no longer retain water. It is therefore necessary to pour a little on to the top surface each day or two.

FILLING OASIS WITH WATER

The blocks when bought are dry and very light, but they are easily filled with water. Cut a block, using a knife, into a shape to fit the container. It should be sufficiently large to hold the number of stems used in the design but rarely needs to be bigger than about 5″ × 5″ and a smaller block is normally used. If the Oasis sticks up above the container, stems can be pushed in to flow downwards attractively. Drop the cut block into a sink of water which is deeper than the block and remove it when it sinks to the level of the water which takes about ten to twenty minutes. It is then fully soaked and ready for use. It cannot absorb too much water by leaving it to soak longer.

Holding Stems in Position

Stems may be dropped into a container without any more support than the neck of the container but it is often difficult to keep the flower heads separated so that each flower can be seen. Using a supporting device means less flowers are necessary for a pleasing design, and the methods are quite simple.

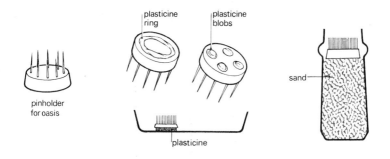

A PINHOLDER Stems are impaled on the pins or slipped between them. Push the stem straight down and then angle it by gently pressing. This support is good for simple designs especially those which include woody branches and few flowers. Stems are held accurately in position but it is not as easy to place them in a sideways position for which Oasis is better.

Containers with pinholders, the taller one uses sand

Containers with Oasis. Wire netting, held in place with rubber bands, can give extra support

WIRE NETTING 2″ mesh is crumpled into a ball leaving spaces to insert stems and is placed into the cavity of the container. A rubber band is put around the netting and container together as otherwise the wire netting slips about. This is also prevented by placing a pinholder in the container below the netting and pushing a stem through the netting on to the pinholder. It is a type of support which is better for arrangements using many flowers and leaves. The netting size can usually be estimated by cutting a square piece about twice the width of the container in each direction. If the cut ends are left standing up out of the container they can be used for winding around long flower stems for added support.

OASIS This provides very accurate support as well as water but is more suitable for arrangements using many stems. When used in a simple design the Oasis may be harder than a pinholder to conceal and it is not especially attractive in appearance. Being heavy with water Oasis does not normally slip about. If it does not exactly fit the container then a wide pinned pinholder can be used which is especially made for holding Oasis in position. Normal pinholders become very clogged up if used for this purpose. Oasis cannot be used indefinitely as it eventually crumbles because of the many holes made in it. It is consequently a more expensive support than wire netting or a pinholder.

PLASTICINE A roll or several blobs of plasticine or Bostik can be placed on to the bottom of a *dry* pinholder. The pinholder is placed on to a *dry* container, and given a slight twist. This attaches the pinholder and prevents it from slipping.

FLORIST'S REEL WIRE This is useful in place of rubber bands for holding wire netting in place. Cut a length and push it through one of the holes in the wire netting. Twist the end around the wire of the netting and secure the other end similarly to any handle or stem on the container. This can be repeated using another length of wire for extra stability. A piece of wire netting used as a 'cap' can give a second support to stems placed in Oasis. This is helpful to beginners who may put stems in and out of the Oasis rather often, an action which makes large holes and causes the stems to slip about. The wire netting 'cap' prevents this.

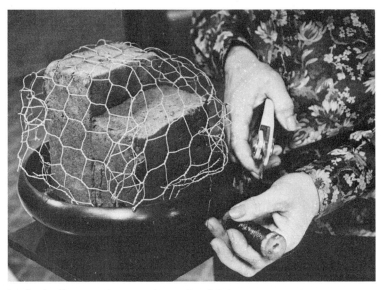

Mechanics for supporting stems in a pedestal design

Hiding the Supports

Wire, Oasis and pinholders are not usually attractive to look at and should be concealed. Wire netting or Oasis used in arrangements containing many flowers can be concealed with leaves cut with very short stems. It is often helpful to place these in position to cover the supports before doing the arrangement.

Simple designs arranged on a pinholder can appear cluttered when leaves are placed all over the pinholder to hide it. Other cover-ups are more attractive and do not spoil the simplicity of the design and they can be stones, small pieces of driftwood, shattered windscreen glass, shells, pieces of coral, moss, pebbles.

Design

There are innumerable combinations of flowers, foliage, fruits, driftwood, containers, accessories and bases. This makes flower arrangement an absorbing interest – there is always a variety of colours, textures and shapes to combine and something new to try. The transient quality of plant material provides a constant,

19

fascinating challenge to the arranger, but designs should be assembled quickly and not laboured. They may not look perfect but another arrangement can be done in a few days and improvements may then be made. Flower Arrangement clubs, Horticultural Societies and classes for flower arrangement in Colleges of Further Education are available over almost all Britain for those who wish to learn more and to meet, in friendly surroundings, others with a similar interest. There are also many books on both flower arrangement and gardening for those who wish to study at home.

Meanwhile, practice and experience are wonderful teachers and very lovely arrangements can be made for the home without extensive knowledge. There are a few guidelines on which to concentrate but no rules.

1 Leave space around every flower, however full the design, as only by doing this can the shape of the flower be clearly seen.
2 Place the flowers around a central axis in the way that branches can grow from a central tree trunk as this gives a natural appearance. If the stem ends are kept close together on whichever type of support is used there is a graceful sense of radiation from a central point.
3 Cut stems different lengths as this means the flowers can be more easily seen. Gardeners sometimes flinch at the cutting of stems and many flower arrangers do cut stems too short but reasonable cutting is necessary for a pleasing design.
4 Make the plant material more important than the container so that the flowers are not overwhelmed and insignificant.
5 Turn the flowers slightly to face different ways. An arrangement of many flowers should have a few facing forwards in the centre with the others gradually turning away so that all sides of the flower are seen, even the backs, which can also be beautiful.
6 Choose flowers, leaves and a container related in size.
7 Use a variety of colours which can be more attractive than using only one or two. Repeat each colour used to give a link and keep if possible to a colour key – all subtle or rich or pale or brilliant.
8 Add contrasts in textural surfaces and in shapes to give more interest.
9 Use leaves to 'stretch' the flowers.

Line and Mass Designs

The two main groups of design are line and mass, however these are very broad classifications and there are many inbetweens. Mass designs use many flowers and leaves and the outline shape is emphasized. It may follow a circle or a triangle (and there are other shapes) but the beauty is of massed colour and texture. Line designs are sparser and long shapes such as bare branches are dominant in the design. There is far more space in line designs so that individual shapes can be clearly seen and the

A line arrangement with one garden lily, a bare branch and arum leaves

A mass arrangement of annuals in a plant saucer and pot which has been painted with green chalkboard paint containing sand for a rough texture

outline is not solid as in a mass arrangement. Both styles are beautiful in different ways and whereas line is especially good in winter when flowers are scarce, mass designs are lovely when flowers are more freely available in summer. The more you arrange flowers the more you find that you can use less in a design than you imagined at first, and this pleases the gardener in the family.

Suiting Your Home

Flowers bring a happy and welcoming feeling to a home, giving a cared-for impression. Somehow the house seems more furnished and is certainly more colourful when bowls of flowers are placed here and there. Some thought should be given to the position in which they are placed. Many traditional homes have niches in the walls where ornaments may stand and these can be adapted to hold a flower arrangement instead. The hall table is a good place providing a gay welcome, as long as the design does not get in the way of the other things which belong on a hall table. Dark corners can be brought to life with light flowers. The table used for seated meals always looks better when it displays a flower arrangement, even if only a few flowers are placed in a small container. Sideboards, fireplaces in summer, coffee tables, dressing tables, mantelpieces, shelves, free-standing pedestals are all excellent positions for flowers. Hot positions such as in a sunny window, the top of the television set, over a radiator, on a mantelpiece when a fire is burning should be avoided as the heat shortens the life of the cut flower. Arrangements should suit their settings in style, size, colour and shape so that they seem totally in harmony with their surroundings.

Containers

After making arrangements in the suggested basic containers and when supporting the flowers becomes easy, try other containers as there are many receptacles which can be used – old teapots, glasses, soup tureens, gravy boats, baskets lined with a tin, jugs, bowls are just a few possibilities.

The container and the plant material should appear as one design with the plant material and not two separate parts. The container will blend more easily with the flowers if its colour is neutral such as grey, brown, black, dull green. Brilliant colours can be distracting and white can appear too dominant unless white is also present in the plant material.

Preserving Plant Material

Some plant material can be preserved with glycerine which is absorbed into the stem taking the place of water. The leaves normally turn brown but there are many lovely shades and they may last for years. Foliage treated in this way is invaluable in the winter for combining with a few fresh flowers and is not harmed by being placed in water. It is also attractive painted and glittered for Christmas designs.

Recipe
Mix well together one part glycerine to two parts hot water.

A bottle of glycerine can be bought from any chemist and poured into a wide-necked jar. The same bottle should be filled twice over with very hot water and the solution well stirred. Place the stem ends in the mixture at once. It should be topped up later if necessary so that the stem end is in about 1″ of the mixture until the plant material has completely changed colour. The length of time varies from a few days to three months and preservation is complete when there is no green remaining. The plant material should be groomed beforehand so that glycerine is not wasted on damaged leaves.

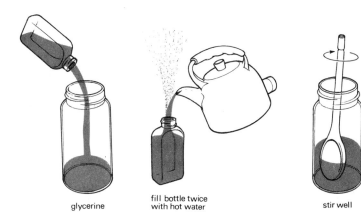

glycerine | fill bottle twice with hot water | stir well

Remove crowded leaves, damaged leaves and lower leaves. Split and scrape the stem end.

keep mixture at a level of 2"

submerge leaves which absorb moisture slowly

mop large tough leaves

Young foliage and leaves turning colour in the Autumn do not take glycerine well and middle-aged leaves are the most successful. July is a good month for preservation. Very tough leaves, such as ivy, should be mopped with the glycerine mixture before the stem ends are placed in it. This prevents them drying out before the glycerine travels to the extremities. Alternatively small leaves may be submerged in the mixture. Lighter colours may be obtained by placing the preserved plant material in strong sunshine to fade.

Drying

Plant material may be dried but the results are more fragile than preservation by absorption of glycerine. There are several methods and in each one plant material should be picked on a dry day, in perfect condition and just before maturity. The lists at the end of each chapter indicate the best method for each variety of plant.

DRYING BY HANGING UP

This is suitable for stems with rigid tissues such as achillea, delphinium, larkspur and many stems carrying seedpods. Hang the cut plant material upside down in small bunches in a warm, dry place until it feels quite dry. Foliage should be removed as this shrivels. Dried flowers can be used in water with fresh ones

Grasses and seedheads may be sprayed with hair lacquer or clear varnish to prevent blowing

The stems of small, dried seedheads and flowers may be pushed into a foam cone, or secured with a long pin

if the ends are sealed by dipping them in nail polish or melted candlewax but are more successful used in dry supports.

DRYING BY PRESSING

This flattens the plant material but otherwise the shape is retained. It is suitable for flowers and leaves that are not thick or succulent. They should be placed between two sheets of blotting paper, under a carpet or a heavy book or in a flower press, made or bought for this purpose. Flowers and leaves with heavy tissue pressed in this way may be used in arrangements but the more delicate plant material is better used in framed flower pictures and pressed by the glass against the background which should be covered with paper or fabric. Copydex is the best adhesive for this and only small spots of it are necessary.

Making a pressed flower picture

A completed pressed flower picture

Macleaya cordata, *the smaller leaves are a good shape
for pressing*

DRYING WITH A DESICCANT

Silica gel, sand, borax and alum are desiccants which withdraw
moisture from flowers or leaves buried in them. Silica gel acts
quickly and will dry a flower in 3 to 4 days. This is suitable for
three dimensional flowers such as roses. If flowers with fine
petals are used, the silica gel should be ground down with a roll-
ing pin otherwise its heaviness spoils the shape. Place a flower
with the stem cut off, on about 1″ of silica gel, in a tin or box.
Pour on more of the desiccant until the flower is covered. Place
a cover on the tin and put it into the airing cupboard. When
removing the flower take great care as the results are very fragile.
False stems are normally necessary as the flower stems shrivel.
Turn a small hook down on the end of a stubwire (bought from
a florist), push the other end down through the centre of the
flower and draw the hook into the flower centre. This is better

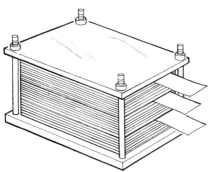

flower press

drying with a desiccant

leaf

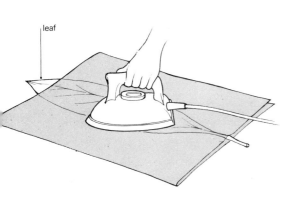

water

drying hydrangea

29

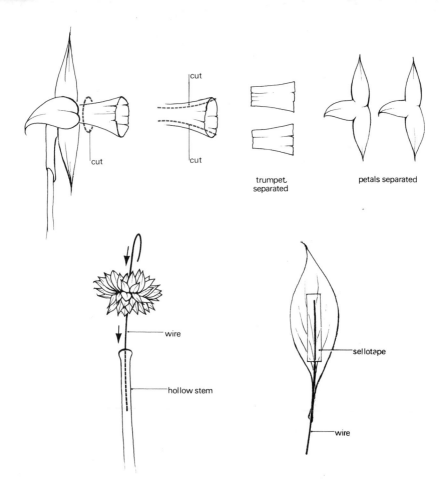

cut

cut

cut

cut

trumpet
separated

petals separated

wire

hollow stem

sellotape

wire

done before burying it in the desiccant and the wire can be bent over whilst drying takes place. The wire 'stem' may be disguised by binding with florists tape or by slipping it into a hollow stem.

All dried plant material should be stored in a dry place as otherwise it re-absorbs moisture.

2 Roses

The beauty of a rose is irresistible and it is the most loved of all flowers. It is also easy to grow and its popularity increases every year and all over the world. When an exciting new rose arrives on the scene, and this happens frequently, it is heralded, fêted and discussed as a new star on the football field. According to archaeologists roses have existed for at least thirty million years and it is believed to have been the first flower brought under cultivation. There is evidence that a garden rose was cultivated in Greece in the 5th century B.C. and the Romans used them lavishly, spreading them like carpets on the ground and wreathing their heads with them during revelries. Ancreon, a poet of the 6th century B.C. hailed the rose as 'the boon of the earth' and ever since it has been acclaimed by many civilizations. It became the emblem of the early church and the chosen badge of many kings. Throughout the ages it has been the most romantic of flowers and its praises have been sung by many poets and writers – Shakespeare mentioned it no less than seventy times. Perhaps no-one has loved roses more than Josephine, the first wife of Napoleon I. She planted one of every known variety in her garden at Malmaison near Paris and commissioned Pierre-Joseph Redouté to paint many of them. This he did with unequalled delicacy and charm and 170 are included in a remarkable book *Les Roses* published in the early 19th century.

It is surprising that a flower with so much beauty can be grown with a minimum amount of work – no wonder it is so popular. It provides abundant growth more quickly than any other shrub and a good supply of flowers is the happy result of a little basic care, which is not difficult to understand or apply even if you are a very new gardener.

A pedestal arranagement of summer flowering perennials including delphiniums, phlox, *Thalictrum flavum*, daisies and leaves of *Hosta crispula*. Arranged by Molly Duerr

Foliage which has been treated with glycerine turns many shades of brown, L. untreated green foliage and a foxglove seedhead, R. treated plant material.

Growing Roses

Buying Rose Bushes

WHERE TO BUY

It is important to buy roses from a reputable nursery or garden centre. So-called 'bargains' from other sources and those given as free issues with food coupons, are not reliable although there is nothing wrong with collections offered at reduced rates if they are bought from good suppliers. A rose has a life span normally of 15–20 years so it is worth buying a strong healthy plant in the first place and one that you really like because of its colour, shape and maybe fragrance. There are many varieties and it is easy to be spoilt for choice.

WHEN TO BUY

It is easier to choose roses for your own garden at a time when they can be seen in bloom elsewhere and a visit to a garden open to the public, a garden centre, park, nursery or flower show is well worthwhile from June to September. On older plants you can consider

1 the colour, shape and fragrance of the flowers;
2 the height and spread of the bush;
3 the strength of the stems;
4 the quality of the foliage;
5 the abundance of flowers;
6 the resistance to bad weather;
7 the habit of growth.

Orders can then be placed for those you select and they will be delivered in the Autumn or Spring. For those who want an 'instant' garden there are container grown roses which can be bought at any time and planted all the year round, even when in flower.

The alternative to seeing roses in bloom is to select them from an illustrated catalogue which can be obtained, normally free of

An arrangement of modern roses with the old shape in brown, peach and mauve, Japanese honeysuckle and grey-leaved Rosa rubrifolia

charge, from suppliers. Pictures of roses give some idea of colour and shape but are not as reliable as seeing the actual flower and it is easy to become carried away by glowing descriptions only to be disappointed when the bush chosen and nurtured appears in flower.

Planting Roses

WHEN TO PLANT

Roses are normally planted from mid-October, which is the best time, until the end of March. This is when there is minimum growth and the disturbance of a removal from one place to another does the bush little harm. Container grown roses may be planted at any time providing the soil is not sodden or frozen. Care should be taken that the soil around the roots is not disturbed when the plastic container is removed for planting.

Roses may be delivered at a time when the ground is not suitable for planting although nurserymen do try to fit in with the weather. Bad weather is no time for the gardener to be out or the bush to be planted and if wrapped in damp newspaper and stored in a frost free shed or garage, the rose can be kept for a better day. Planting should not be delayed longer than necessary.

THE SITE

Roses may be planted in beds restricted to roses, which gives a rather formal appearance, or they may be combined with other plants. Some people like to grow only one variety in a bed but this needs a large garden and in order to provide a large choice of colour and shape for cutting for the house, flower arrangers usually prefer a mixture of many varieties. I am happy to have a riot of colour in one bed and I like to plant new roses as they appear on the market amongst the existing bushes. With a little planning consideration can be given to grouping colours and using a variety of height.

Whether grown separately or combined with other plants roses do need an open position, sheltered if possible from draughts and away from shady trees. Climbing and rambling roses need a wall, fence or pole to which they can be tied as they do not climb of their own accord. Large shrub roses usually look better when combined with other shrubs in a border as they take up a lot of room in a rose bed.

PREPARATION OF THE SOIL

Roses thrive in most soils but dislike chalk and very peaty soils. A moist slightly acid fertile soil is ideal. When the site has been decided the bed needs some preparation before planting time.

NEW BEDS

Digging is necessary (and excellent exercise) because it improves the texture of the soil. Dig over the site and remove all weeds paying particular attention to perennials such as thistles and couch-grass. Leave the rough ground to settle and weather for about a month and then fork and rake the surface so that the soil is crumbly and level. It is then ready for planting.

OLD BEDS

Old rose-beds may have become 'rose sick' after growing nothing else for about ten years. In this case it is better to start a new bed elsewhere and to grow different plants in the old bed or to turf it over. Alternatively if there is no other suitable site for roses the old soil can be exchanged to a depth of about 10″ with soil from another part of the garden which has not previously grown roses. Again leave the ground to settle before raking smooth. Single bushes need the soil dug in the same way before planting.

HOW TO PLANT

New roses can be pruned before planting (see page 37). If the roots seem very dry when the rose arrives at your home, soak them in a bucket of water for an hour before planting. Then dig

a hole in the rosebed or border large enough for the roots to be spread out horizontally and not squashed together (it is a temptation to push them together for speed). There is a knob, called the union, on the main stem just above the roots. This is where the new plant was budded on to the stock by the nurseryman. The union should be just under the top of the soil after the rose is firmly planted. This may be difficult to judge but an easy method of finding the correct position is to place a cane across the hole so that it rests on the bed at either side and to hold the rose, as it is planted, so that the union is immediately under the cane.

Bonemeal and peat should be included at planting time. Put peat into a bucket and moisten it with water and bonemeal into a second bucket. Scatter one handful of bonemeal and two or three handfuls of moist peat amongst the roots as you replace the soil around the rose. Shake the bush occasionally so that the soil finds its way between the roots and finally push down with your foot on the surface of the soil all around the roots so that the bush is planted firmly in the ground and cannot be uprooted on a windy day.

Roots should be spread out when planting

A cane measures the planting depth

Container grown roses should have the plastic container cut off and keeping the soil around the roots intact, the bush should be placed in the hole so that the top of this soil is at the same level as the bed. It is important to make sure that the soil in the container is moist before planting.

DISTANCE APART

To allow for growth rose bushes should be planted with the main stems about $1\frac{1}{2}'$ to $2'$ apart. Big shrub roses should have about $4'$ between each one and climbers and ramblers should be not less than $6'$ apart.

Pruning Roses

A rose will certainly continue to grow and bloom for several years without pruning but it will gradually deteriorate and the flowers will become much smaller. A rose keeps renewing itself with new shoots while the older ones become weak or die, unlike a tree which continues to grow up and on. It is important that these new shoots receive all the energy of the plant and that

A rose bush firmly planted

it is not wasted on old shoots which are becoming less productive. For this reason the old, weak shoots are removed by pruning when the plant is resting between the Autumn and early Spring.

There is no need to keep to a definite date for pruning or to do it in bad weather because you feel it must be done. Prune some time in March on a day when it is a pleasure to be outside.

Use a pair of sharp secateurs or pruners. Long-arm pruners are the easiest to use on such a thorny plant. It is sensible to wear thick gardening gloves for this prickly job. Do not get anxious about pruning – it is not the end of the world or the bush to cut it in the wrong place!

Remove
1 Dead wood – this looks brittle and is usually grey/brown. Keep cutting away until greenish/white wood is reached or the base of the bush.
2 Weak stems which look very thin compared with other stems.
3 Branches growing from the centre of the bush.
4 Part of all the remaining stems as this encourages them to grow strongly. They can have hard, medium or light pruning and this depends on the type of rose and the results desired. Harder pruning means bigger flowers but there will be less of them. Remove some of each remaining stem as follows
Hard pruning, two-thirds
Medium pruning, half
Light pruning, one-third

These stems should be cut $\frac{1}{4}''$ above a bud. A bud appears as a small swelling with a semi-circular scar beneath it. Buds give rise to new shoots and if you prune in late Spring small sproutings of leaves may have already appeared. The cut should be made on a slant. To keep the centre of the bush free of stems cut above an outward facing bud and knock off any lower shoots which may have appeared and which point into the centre of the bush.

Prune above a bud

PRUNING DIFFERENT TYPES OF ROSE –
NEW ROSES

Hard prune to about 3" above the union. This is easier to do in the hand before planting the bush (and also saves one's back). Container grown roses need not be pruned until the following Spring.

HYBRID TEA ROSES

As a child I thought this term referred to roses which surrounded elegant ladies when they took afternoon tea but have found since that 'tea' is derived in this instance from the scent of the bruised fresh tea leaf, the first tea rose to be introduced being 'Hume's Blush tea-scented China rose'. This description has persisted despite the many fragrances now in existence.

Hybrid tea roses have large shapely, usually double flowers with a high pointed centre. Flowers are produced singly or in small clusters from June to October with two peak flowering periods around July and September. A modern example is 'Peace'. Medium or hard pruning.

39

FLORIBUNDAS

This is easy to remember if you think of many (or an abundance of) flowers. The flowers are smaller than those of hybrid tea roses but are produced in large clusters. Some have single flowers, others double but there is a great variety of form and they may be flat, loosely formed, in rosettes, or high centred as a hybrid tea rose. An example is 'Queen Elizabeth'. Medium pruning.

SHRUB ROSES

These are vigorous bushy roses with many of the characteristics of floribundas. They often grow 5′ or more in height. Old-fashioned roses raised before the twentieth century are included in this group but they usually bloom only once whereas many of the later varieties bloom twice. An example is 'Nevada' Light pruning.

CLIMBING ROSES

The long fairly stiff stems need to be tied to something for support. They can be trained up walls, pergolas, fences, screens, pillars and trees. They resemble hybrid tea roses with the exception of the longer stems. An example is 'Handel'. No pruning should be done the first year or a climber could revert to the smaller form, but afterwards prune lightly. Rambler roses also have smaller, often rosette shaped flowers. An example is 'Albertine'. Light pruning.

MINIATURES

These are tiny replicas of hybrid tea or floribunda roses, and are about 8″ in height. An example is 'Baby Masquerade'. Medium pruning.

STANDARD ROSES

These are hybrid tea or floribunda roses which have been budded by the nurseryman on to a straight briar stem. They are usually about 4′ in height and look like a small tree in shape with a head of branches at the top. Any shoots appearing from the main stem will be suckers and should be removed. Hard or medium pruning.

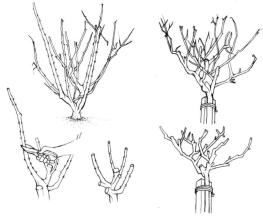

Hybrid tea rose   Standard rose

Shrub rose

Suckers

Suckers are shoots which grow from the roots and also from the main stem below the branches. They are recognizable because they look quite different from other shoots. The stems are thinner and the leaves are smaller and normally a different green from the rest of the leaves on the bush. Suckers are shoots growing

41

A sucker on a standard rose

from the old bush on which the new one was started and if they are allowed to continue growing they produce small single flowers (wild roses) which eventually take over the whole bush. It is important that they are removed as soon as possible and completely. Pull them off the bush from the place where they started growing. It may be necessary to scrape away soil to do this. If they are stubborn and will not pull off then cut them away close to the bush.

Mulch

Apply a mulch spread over the roots, about 1″ or more thick, in May when the soil has warmed up. Moist peat is easy to obtain and apply. If you feel extravagant spread it over the whole bed as it discourages the growth of weeds.

Weeds

Weeds can be prevented if a liberal mulch is applied. If any pop through they can be pulled out by hand or with a small fork or hoe. Alternatively there is a special weedkiller on the market which can be applied to rose beds. It prevents the weeds from growing without harming the roses. It cannot be used for beds which contain any other plants or they will also die. Apply according to the instructions on the packet in early Spring after clearing the beds of weeds. As a result no weeds will appear in the rose-beds all summer. This saves a lot of work and you can lie in the sun in July enjoying the tidy, weedless, rose beds without any conscience.

Underplanting

Most modern roses do not suffer in any way if plants are grown under them. This is useful in a small garden where there is little planting space for roses alone. The plants should be not more than 24" in height when fully grown so that the roses are not overshadowed. There can be no underplanting if a weedkiller is used on the rose beds. Hybrid tea roses are not very beautiful bushes to look at and they are grown for the flowers not the shape of the bush so underplanting can soften the appearance of the bushes. It is sensible to grow plants under the roses, which can also be cut for arranging in the house. Suggestions:
Hostas of the smaller leafed varieties

H. albomarginata
H. fortunei 'Aurea'
H. lancifolia
H. undulata

Alchemilla mollis (lady's mantle). This has useful round green leaves and small yellow-green flowers which look attractive with roses.
Spring-flowering bulbs such as hyacinths, crocuses, scillas, chionadoxas, tulips with short stems, miniature daffodils
Forget-me-nots
Nepeta (Catmint)
Tellima grandiflora (false alum root). The rounded, scallop-edged leaf is useful for arrangements and is often mottled with brown in the Autumn. The flowers are tall and wand like but will not shadow the roses.
Ruta graveolens (rue). This is a neat blue-green shrub which is evergreen but it may not be hardy in some districts.
Pansies and violas

Vinca major 'Variegata' (variegated periwinkle). This provides useful trailing foliage.

Bergenia cordifolia (pigsqueak). The leaves often go reddish in the Autumn and are invaluable larger leaves for flower arrangement.

Stachys lanata (lamb's ear). 'Silver carpet' is non-flowering, evergreen or rather 'ever-grey' as the leaves are a furry-grey in colour.

Anaphalis yedoensis (pearly everlasting). This has small white flowers which dry well for winter use.

Salvia argentea (silver clary). This is a biennial but if the flowers are cut out each year it may become a perennial. The leaves are large and silver/white.

Feeding Roses

Most plants, as children, grow better when well fed and this is especially true of the rose. New roses should not be given any food during their first summer other than the bonemeal added at planting time but all other roses need feeding three times a year.

1 In early Spring and before applying the mulch, scatter two handfuls of bonemeal over each square yard (approximately) of the rose beds at any time.

2 In May or early June before mulching and again at the end of July, immediately before the roses are at their best, give the bushes 'a good meal' of a quicker acting fertilizer so that there will be a large number of lovely flowers. There are specially blended fertilizers on the market for roses and the manufacturers instructions should be followed. Normally about a handful should be scattered over each square yard or around each rose bush if planted singly.

If the ground is dry, water the fertilizer in but do not work it into the soil with a tool as this may damage the roots and cause suckers to grow.

Pests and Diseases

Pests and diseases can attack roses and spoil their appearance as cut flowers or weaken the plant's growth. Some roses are more susceptible than others. Prevention is easier than cure and spraying is easy. Buy a small handspray and a special preparation for roses which includes insecticide to prevent insects and

Spraying a climbing rose

fungicide to prevent diseases. This is a 'cocktail' but each can be applied separately. In either case mix according to the manu-facturers instructions and spray all over the bush usually three times – in May, July and late August.

Deadheading

This simply means removing faded flowers and it encourages a second crop to grow on bushes which flower more than once. The easiest way to do this is to cut the stems and let them fall into a basket or bucket which saves untidy beds.

Calendar

October to March	Plant (container grown roses at anytime)
March	Prune (new roses at planting time but not climbers)
	Feed with bonemeal
May	Feed with rose fertilizer
	Mulch and spray
July	Feed with rose fertilizer
	Spray
August	Spray

45

Arranging Roses

Roses are especially easy flowers to arrange and they have been used for decoration for centuries. They are seen in many Renaissance paintings in a variety of vases, and often with the Madonna. They spill out of lovely glass and metal bowls and urns in Flemish and Dutch flower paintings and in neat designs beside lovely, aristocratic ladies in French portraits. Every civilization has cut roses to place them indoors to be admired and enjoyed.

There is a great variety of colour, size, shape and fragrance and no other flower is as successful as the rose arranged with its own buds and leaves. They seem made for each other and do not need the addition of flowers and leaves from other plants. They are equally lovely when arranged in a mass of many varieties or when two or three are placed simply in a container so that their individual beauty can be admired.

Garden roses are so much lovelier when arranged than bought roses and they seem to spill out of the container with elegance and charm. Maybe the stems have a more curving grace but a cut glass vase containing very long stiff stems with small blobs of colour at the top – 'a film star's dressing-room look!' is so much less attractive than a traditional bowl of garden roses. My own preference is for old shrub roses and the modern roses with an old shape – a more rounded and flatter form of flower than those with a high centre and turned back petals which I find rather angular in appearance. The rounded form has a softer beauty in arrangements, but the more angular ones can be effective in modern designs. There are modern shrub roses such as the beautiful pink 'Constance Spry' which have the old shape but also the vigour and health of the new roses. I am delighted every time a rose of this type appears on the market. The flowers are as lovely when full-blown as when in bud, which is more than can always be said of their angular relations.

Cutting

Cutting roses for arranging in the house is good for the bush which is an encouraging thought for the keen flower arranger. It persuades the rose to give a second crop of flowers and eliminates the need for deadheading. Cut stems of only 6″ in length from new bushes during the first summer but longer stems can be cut from established bushes. Cut about half the length of the shoot and this will encourage strong new growth on the remaining stem. Cut on a slant just above a well developed leaf as where the leaf joins the stem there may be a growth bud which will produce another stem and flower. The slanting cut is good for the rose bush and also for the cut flower as more of the inner tissue of the stem is exposed to water in the container.

Cut roses which are in bud so that the flower lasts longer in the house; but the bud should show some colour as all-green buds sometimes fail to open in the house. Avoid cutting if possible in the middle of a hot dry day as the bush will be low in water and the cut flower will need a lot of filling up. Take a bucket half-full of warm water (a full bucket slops over and can wet you) and place the cut stem in this at once. The rose stem can easily absorb air which prevents water from entering and consequently the flower will then wilt quickly. If roses are cut and cannot be placed in water at once they should be recut before placing in water to remove any air bubble. About an inch of stem should be removed and more if it has been out of water for long.

Conditioning

1 Snip off with flower scissors the lower thorns and the lower leaves on the stem which would be under water when the rose is arranged. These become decayed under water. A stripper is sold which can be drawn down the stems to remove both thorns and leaves.
2 Cut the stem end upwards for an inch as rose stems have a hard exterior and cutting exposes more of the inner tissue to water.
3 After removing the thorns and lower leaves and cutting the stems upwards, replace the stems in the bucket which should be filled with tepid water. Leave the roses to soak in this in a cool place away from draughts and strong light for about two hours. This fills the stems with water before arranging in the shallower water of a decorative container. The many petals of a rose flower transpire (lose water to the atmosphere) rapidly and water can be lost more quickly than the stem can take it

up. Spraying with a fine mist of water when the arrangement is completed is helpful.

Rambler roses last such a short time in the house that they are hardly worth cutting. Old roses also have rather a short life – perhaps only two days but this depends on the heat of the room. Hybrid tea roses last the longest as cut flowers. Leaves used alone last better if cut with a section of hard stem.

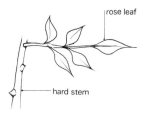

WILTED ROSES

A rose may flop before the end of its life through lack of water in the stem. The bend often occurs at the top of the stem. Remove the rose from the arrangement, recut the stem end to remove any hard seal or air bubble and float the rose flower, leaves and stem, in a sink of tepid water for about two hours. The flower should soon perk up again. If a sink is not available, cutting the stem end and placing it in warm water often helps. Very long stems should be cut quite short so that the water reaches the bend at the top of the stem quickly.

floating a wilted flower

Retarding Roses

The development of a flower can be retarded if it is needed for a special occasion some time after cutting or if a bunch of roses is needed with flowers open at different stages, such as tight buds, half-open and open flowers. Place buds wrapped in polythene into the refrigerator for a few days. Recut the stem end and place in warm water to start development again. Roses sometimes last in the garden well into late Autumn and it is possible to hold some in the refrigerator for Christmas.

Mechanics

Roses can be arranged successfully on a pinholder, in plastic foam, wire netting or any combination of these. The hard stems push easily on to a pinholder and are inserted without any trouble into plastic foam.

Preserving

Rose leaves take glycerine well. Cut the leaf on a section of hard stem and place the stem end in the glycerine mixture for about two weeks. The flowers can be dried in silica gel and take about three or four days to dry. Single roses can be pressed or rose petals may be removed from the flower, pressed and then re-assembled when sticking.

Design

The rose is an easy flower to arrange with its own leaves because it has long slender buds which can be placed on the outside of the arrangement, fully open rounded flowers for emphasis in the centre and leaves and half-open flowers for variety and gradual change between the buds and open flowers. The leaves make excellent covering for the mechanics. Single roses which open to show the stamens in the centre have a special charm as the rough-looking stamens make a happy contrast with the smooth petals.

STYLES

Roses tend, because of their long history, to be associated with

The rose 'Queen Elizabeth' arranged in a hearth by Dorothy Haworth

period and traditional styles of flower arrangement and look lovely in a mass design. Two or three roses can look dramatic in more modern designs combined with driftwood or cane but they are rarely suitable in abstract designs because of their natural and traditional appearance.

COMBINING WITH OTHER PLANT MATERIAL

This is unnecessary as the rose is so effective arranged with its own foliage and buds but sometimes flowers and leaves of a visually rough texture are pleasing. The early flowers of sedum, which are green before turning pink or red, carnations, dried achillea and preserved beech leaves enhance the silky texture of rose flowers.

Colours are a matter of personal preference, as there are so many from which to choose that it is sensible to grow roses in colours which you know will suit the furnishings of your home and with which you enjoy living. There are roses in white, yellow, orange, red, violet and many inbetween shades, tones and tints such as cream, apricot, pink, brown, maroon, mauve. There are no blue roses, and I am not sure I should like it if there were, but there is a green one called *Rosa chinensis viridiflora*. It is very small and not really much like a rose in appearance but it is useful as a filler-in. Green, grey, bronze, red, yellow and beige (preserved) foliage may be used with roses depending on the general colour scheme. Some of the brilliant colours of the modern hybrid tea roses are difficult to take in a mass and can be tiring on the eye, and they are better arranged in twos or threes.

CONTAINERS

Traditional and period containers always suit roses. The range of oranges, apricots, pinks and browns look lovely in copper. Yellows and oranges suit brass. Pale pink and mauve roses with

'Peace' rose combined with glycerined Fatshedera *leaves and coconut palm spathes, found on holiday, arranged by Molly Duerr*

51

grey foliage are perfect for silver. Containers in the earth colours of browns, greys and greens always look right with roses of any colour. Old roses are in complete harmony with antique containers, especially in a traditionally furnished home.

Old shrub roses known by Empress Josephine

A Selection of Roses for Planting and Arranging

The list could fill a complete book but the following are a few of the many available which are reliable for arranging in various styles and in different colour schemes

HT Hybrid tea
Fl Floribunda
C   Climber
Sh Shrub

WHITE AND CREAM

Iceberg (Fl) pure white, bud tinged with pink, weather resistant
Pascali (HT) white shaded cream, usually one flower to a stem

YELLOWS

Peace (HT) light clear yellow edged with pale pink, large flowers and bush, weather resistant
Grandpa Dickson (HT) yellow fading to cream, weather resistant

ORANGES

Soraya (HT) deep orange with blackish shading becoming bluish-mauve, long stems, weather resistant
Cairngorm (Fl) bright orange
Helen Taubel (HT) delicate apricot-pink
Whisky Mac (HT) gold overlaid with tangerine and bronze
Sutter's Gold (HT) light orange shaded red
Lady Sylvia (HT) light pink with yellow base

REDS

Topsi (Fl) orange-scarlet, free-flowering
Super Star (HT) light vermillion without shading, weather resistant
Fragrant Cloud (HT) softer red, good shape, weather resistant
Ernest H. Morse (HT) rich red, weather resistant
Crimson Wave (Fl) 2 tone red, opening to show stamens
Fervid (Fl) scarlet, opening to show stamens

VIOLETS

News (Fl) red-purple with stamens showing when open
Lake Como (Fl) lavendar-lilac, wavy-edged petals, bright yellow centres when open

53

Blue Moon (HT) silvery-lilac
Silver Lining (HT) silvery-rose

PINKS

Wendy Cussons (HT) cerise flushed scarlet, weather resistant
Sea Pearl (Fl) pale pink-apricot, hybrid tea type of stem
Perfecta (HT) palest pink shaded and tipped with rose red
Queen Elizabeth (Fl) clear unshaded pink with long stems
Carol Amling (Fl) small flat flowers of deep rose
Dearest (Fl) salmon-pink
Fairy Dancers (Fl) small pink-apricot flowers
Chanelle (Fl) cream overlaid peach-pink
Elizabeth Harkness (HT) palest pink

BROWNS (always favourites with flower arrangers)

Amberlight (Fl) golden brown-buff, pretty shape
Café (Fl) beige
Brownie (Fl) a mixture of golden-yellow, pink and bronze
Tom Brown (Fl) two-tone brown, large clusters
Vesper (Fl) burnt orange
Artistic (Fl) golden apricot brown
Fantan (HT) copper bronze
Jocelyn (Fl) reddish-mahogany

OLD SHRUB ROSES

Blanc Double de Coubert (Rugosa Sh) white 5', very fragrant
Boule de Neige (Bourbon Sh) cream-white touched with pink,
    round medium sized flower, very hardy, 6'
Celestial (Alba Sh) clear pink, painted by Redouté, 5', delicate
    charm
Fantin-Latour (Centifolia Sh) pale pink, crinkly and full flower, 5'
Charles de Mills (Gallica Sh) crimson-maroon, good garden rose, 4'
Gloire des Mousseux (centifolia moss Sh) 4', bright pink
William Lobb (Centifolia moss Sh) dark purple, 7'
Louise Odier (Bourbon Sh) camellia shaped flower in soft pink, 6'
Madame Pierre Oger (Bourbon Sh) globular pale pink flowers, 6'
Comte de Chambord (Damascena Sh) pink-lilac, very fragrant, 4'
Cardinal de Richelieu (Gallica Sh) maroon-purple, 4'
Madame Isaac Pereire (Bourbon Sh) purple-crimson, large, 7'
Baroness Rothschild (Hybrid perpetual) pink, 4'
Baronne Prévost (HT) rose pink, large, flat

Souvenir du Docteur Jamain (HT) plum, needs good soil
Königen von Dänemark (Alba Sh) soft pink, 6'
Madame Hardy (Damascena Sh) full white flowers incurved centre petals, 5'
Honorine de Brabant (Bourbon Sh) pale lilac streaked purple, globular flower, looks very old for period arrangements, 6'

CLIMBERS

Cl. Cécile Brunner (China Fl) the sweetheart rose, very small pale pink, perfectly formed miniature flower
Cl. Gloire de Dijon, pale cream shaded orange, seldom without flower, 12'
Compassion (Cl) pale salmon orange
Handel (Cl) cream edged with rose pink, 10'
Danse du Feu (Cl) orange scarlet, 12'
Golden Showers (Cl) pale yellow, 8'
Pink Perpetue (Cl) clear pink, 15'
Parkdirector-Riggers (Cl) good for East and North walls, red, 12'
Zéphirine Drouhin (Bourbon Cl) pink, thornless, 9'

MODERN ROSES WITH AN OLD APPEARANCE

Magenta (F. Sh) rosy magenta, rosette shaped
Lavender Lassie (Sh) lilac to pink, rosette shaped
The Wife of Bath (Sh) pale pink
Gruss an Aachen (Fl) pink fading to cream
Rosemary Rose (Fl) carmine, rosette shaped
Plentiful (Fl) deep pink
Europeana (Fl) red
Constance Spry (Sh) pink, large, rounded flowers
Fritz Nobis (Sh) pale salmon-pink
Agnes (Rugosa) amber-yellow, ball-shaped flowers

ROSES WITH GOOD HEPS (HIPS)

Rosa moyesii 'Geranium', carafe shaped orange-red heps $2\frac{1}{2}$" long
R. Sweginzowii, glossy heps smaller than above
R. rugosa alba, orange-red heps
Fru Dagmar Hartopp, crimson heps
R. x. highdownensis, bunches of heps

MINIATURE ROSES

Baby Masquerade (Min.) peach pink
New Penny (Min.) orange

Cinderella (Min.) very tiny, white
Lavender Lace (Min.) mauve
Perla de Montserrat (Min.) tiny, pink

OTHERS

Rosa chinensis viridiflora, small green streaked brown flowers
R. rubrifolia, mauve-grey foliage
R. omeiensis pteracantha, brown stems with big ruby red thorns
when young. Needs to be hard pruned for red thorns

3 Spring Bulbs

Spring bulbs come almost as high as roses, the top flowers in the popularity poll. This is probably because even the smallest garden can make room for a few tulips or a drift of daffodils and they are ideal for Spring window-boxes, tubs and pots in the house.

> 'A host of golden daffodils;
> Beside the lake, beneath the trees,
> Fluttering and dancing in the breeze'

Random groups of daffodils planted in rough grass

wrote William Wordsworth and there can be few people who are not moved by the sight of their fresh beauty:

> . . . 'And then my heart with pleasure fills
> And dances with the daffodils'

They seem especially precious after the long cold winter, and are a sign that the earth is on the move again. Every Spring I wonder yet again at the way the buds push their way through the hard, frozen ground and burst into flower with such abandon.

What is a Bulb?

Daffodils are bulbous flowers, but not the only ones. There are plants with bulbous and tuberous roots in all families flowering in Spring, Summer and Autumn. The term 'bulb' is often collectively used for plants which have storage organs but they may be corms, tubers or rhizomes, all of which store food and enable the plants to survive long periods without food and water. For this reason they are easy plants to transport and transplant. They can be dug up during the resting period, dried off and moved about with ease.

BULB   This is composed of a number of scales packed tightly together. A good example is the household onion and the scales fall apart as the onion is chopped up.

A CORM   This is a solid storage organ without scales and similar to a thickened stem. It has a membraneous sheath around it and a gladiolus is an example.

A TUBER   This is similar to a corm being solid and without scales but it is also without a sheath. Examples are dahlias and potatoes.

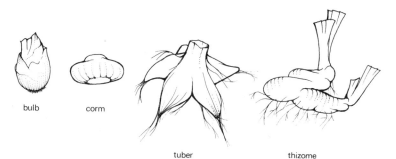

bulb   corm

tuber   thizome

58

A RHIZOME This is an underground root like a stem which sends leafy shoots from the upper surface and roots from the lower side, for example the big bearded iris with sword-like leaves.

This chapter concerns a few of the bulbs which flower in the Spring and early Summer – daffodils, tulips, hyacinths, alliums, irises, all of which die down between June and August. There are many other lovely Spring bulbs such as snowdrop, grape hyacinth, crocus, scilla, fritillary and these are lovely in the garden but have more limited use as cut flowers.

Growing Bulbs

Buying Bulbs

Spring flowering bulbs are on sale from August through the Autumn. As they can be stored without soil they are offered for sale 'dry' during their resting period and will be found by the boxful in nurseries, florists and garden centres. There are bulbs from Holland, Britain and Spain.

A flower can be guaranteed during the first year as it is already in the bulb as an embryo when you buy it. Many commonly grown bulbs are graded by size before they are placed on sale and more must be paid for bigger bulbs, which will produce more, or bigger, flowers. It is a false economy to buy poor stock and well worth the money to buy bulbs of a good size. Some bulbs are expensive because they are new or rare but this is a different matter and there are many less expensive, large bulbs which produce lovely flowers.

The Narcissus Family

Narcissi is the botanical name for a large group of flowers. In general usage the name 'daffodil' is reserved for one with a long trumpet and one with a short cup in the centre is called a 'narcissus'.

Buying

Narcissi are graded according to the number of growing points on the bulb, as these produce flowers.

'single-nosed' bulb   'double nosed' bulb   'mother' bulb

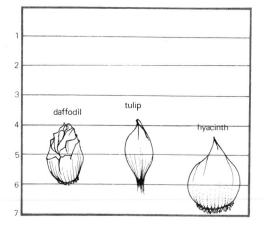

daffodil   tulip   hyacinth

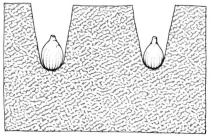

bulbs should rest firmly on the soil at the bottom of the hole

'Single nosed' produces one flower. 'Double nosed' produces two flowers. 'Mother' produces more than two growing points.

DN2 (Double nosed 2) is a good size for garden use.

The Site

Narcissi can be grown in a variety of situations and their great advantage is that lifting each year is unnecessary. They can be left to flower for years without any attention. This makes them suitable for banks and rough grass as well as formal beds. All can grow in full sun or partial shade and in ordinary soil but they thrive if the soil is rich, well manured and protected by slight shade cast by trees or taller plants. However there need be no worries about growing daffodils and one has only to see them flowering in the shallow stony soil of the Lake District to realize that they are not difficult plants.

NATURALIZING

Sacks of narcissi in mixed varieties can be bought at low cost for planting informally – usually known as 'naturalizing' – and there are certain types which are especially suitable. There is one very important consideration when planting narcissi in rough grass – they must be left to die down completely or at least until the leaves are yellowed. This is because the leaves feed the bulb and make sure that it will produce flowers the next season. Cutting off the leaves prematurely may endanger next year's flowers. The grass can look frustratingly untidy and uncared for as the leaves die down but it should not be cut until mid-June. For this reason do decide at planting time if you can stand this untidy appearance for a few weeks in early Summer. Some people tie the leaves up in bundles for neatness but this is not advised as the sun cannot get at enough leaf surface and the food reserves are not formed as well in the bulbs.

OPEN BEDS

Narcissi planted in open beds can be lifted if the untidy look is disliked and if the bed is needed for later flowering plants. Remove the dead flowers but not the stalks and leaves and re-plant in a corner of the garden to die down in peace.

Planting

WHEN TO PLANT

Plant narcissi as soon as they are available in the shops which could be August and this is not too early to plant. They may be planted up until December but the flowers are later and not as satisfactory as when planted earlier.

A natural look is usually more attractive than precise straight lines and a good effect is obtained by simply scattering a handful of bulbs at random on the ground (but don't lose them in long grass). A special tool is made for planting in grass. This cuts a core out of the turf big enough for the bulb which is then dropped into the hole and the turf is replaced. Alternatively small narrow trowels may be used. Planting a drift of daffodils can be a happy family occupation one weekend in August. A full sack soon disappears and everyone enjoys the reward next Spring. A handful of complete fertilizer per square yard can be scattered over the ground at planting time.

When the special tool is not used and the narcissi are planted in beds, the hole made to receive the bulb should be three times the depth of the bulb, for example a 2″ bulb goes into a 6″ hole and will be covered with 4″ of soil. 4″ to 6″ is normal between bulbs.

LIFTING BULBS

This is not necessary unless the beds are wanted, the untidy look is too much or because the bulbs are flowering badly which means they are congested. Lift between July and September, whether in the beds or in a temporary site to which they have been moved, and replant at once. If the bulbs are not flowering well, remove the offsets after lifting and replant them separately. They should flower in one to two years. If for some reason the bulbs cannot be replanted after lifting, dry off in a warm place, remove the leaves by twisting off, also the roots and any soil and keep them dry, but not hot, until they can be replanted.

Narcissi for Growing and Arranging

There are about 8,000 cultivated varieties. The following are reliable and interesting. N denotes good for naturalizing.

Cantatrice	pure white, elegant shape
Charter	lemon, trumpet turns white (expensive at present)

Crinoline	large all white with a frilled edge to the trumpet
Honeybird	pale yellow green with white trumpet
Mrs. Backhouse N	white petals with a pink trumpet
Mount Hood N	white petals and trumpet
Passionale	white petals pink trumpet (expensive)
Spellbinder	clear yellow, trumpet turns white
Trousseau N	white petals yellow trumpet fading to buff
Aruba	cream, yellow cup with orange band
Binkie N	lemon, large cup fades to white
Dove Wings	cream, pale yellow cup
Galway	deep yellow with brighter cup
Geranium	cream petals, orange cup
Kilworth N	white with deep red cup
Pheasants Eye N	classic, white with good eye
Tenby (N. obvallaris)	all yellow, good for naturalizing as it can be left for years

N. asturiensis (syn. N. minimus). This is a miniature yellow daffodil with a 3″ stem which is good for rock gardens and is charming used in naturalistic, landscape arrangements.

Collections can be bought, which include about five varieties, for naturalizing.

Tulips

These are proud, gay flowers with many colours including pure white, almost black, subtle pinks and mauves, vibrant yellows and reds and blended colours. There are also many sizes and lengths of stem from a few inches to 30″ tall. Tulips start flowering soon after the daffodils and have a long season as varieties bloom at different times. The word tulip stems from the Turkish word 'dulband' meaning a turban which has a similar shape to a tulip. They arrived in Europe from Turkey in about 1552 and in England in 1582.

Buying Bulbs

The size is measured in centimetres with good bulbs measuring 10/11 or 11/12 centimetres. Although a good tulip may now be bought for less than four new pence each, the tale was very

Lily-flowered tulips, by courtesy of Pat Brindley

different between 1634 and 1637 in the Low Countries. No other flower has caused so much wild excitement on its arrival and bulbs changed hands at terrific prices. A single bulb of 'Viceroy' was once traded for:

two loads of wheat	four barrels of eight-florin beer
four loads of rye	two barrels of butter
four fat oxen	1,000 pounds of cheese
eight fat pigs	a bed
twelve fat sheep	a suit of clothes
two hogsheads of wine	a silver beaker
	Total: 2,500 florins

'Constance Spry', a modern shrub rose, arranged in an old oil lamp
base.

A simple design for a sideboard of *Achillea filipendulina*
'Coronation Gold', with hosta leaves. Stones cover the pinholder.

A bulb of 'Semper Augustus' was exchanged for twice that much plus a carriage and pair, and one grower once ate a stew which cost him 100,000 florins – his cook had mistaken some of his rare bulbs for onions! The market eventually collapsed because of flooding and a lessening of interest – and this is just as well for us now.

The Site

Although in park beds tulips are planted in rows like soldiers and combined with Spring flowering plants such as wallflowers, they can be extremely attractive in gardens planted in more natural groups of different varieties but in several colours. They may be planted in the front of shrub borders where later annuals or dahlias may replace them. They thrive in an alkaline soil but will grow on an acid one. They do not like shade although light shade is tolerated and a sunny site is preferable. The varieties with short stems are the most suitable for window-boxes and pots.

Planting

WHEN TO PLANT

Late October or early November is the best time. Earlier planting makes tulips more susceptible to disease and the early growth if it starts too soon may be damaged by frost. Although it is not to be recommended, tulips can be planted up to Christmas if stored in a cool place meanwhile.

HOW TO PLANT

Scatter a handful of bonemeal per square yard at planting time and sit the bulbs in position before starting to plant. In this way they can be attractively spaced. Leave about 4″ between each bulb. Make holes with a long narrow trowel and plant the bulb 6″ deep. See that the top of the bulb is at least 4″ below the surface and more than this in light soils.

Deadheading

If the flower has not been cut for use in the house, deadhead as the first petals start to fall by snapping off the head leaving the

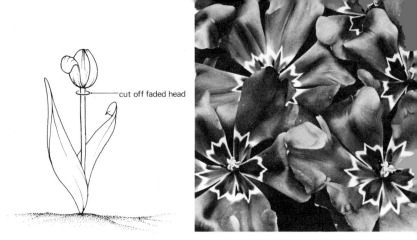

cut off faded head

The centres of tulips can be very exotic and make good emphasis points in an arrangement

stem behind. This helps to manufacture a future flower in the bulb. Some Dutch bulb firms decapitate tulips at the peak of flowering so that good export bulbs will result.

Lifting

Ideally tulips should be lifted. They may be left as perennials and some last a long time but most do not usually like more than two years in any one patch of soil. Lift when the leaves are turning yellow but if the beds are needed for other plants they can be removed to a temporary site until the leaves die down. When lifted, dry off the bulbs in a warm place, clean off old leaves, soil and roots. Discard damaged and diseased bulbs and store the remainder in a cool, dark, airy place on wooden trays until planting time.

Renewal

Some varieties grow on for years but many bulbs do eventually break down, unlike daffodils which go on and on, but new bulbs are inexpensive compared to cut flowers and replacement gives a chance to try newer varieties.

Tulips for Growing and Arranging

There are many varieties of tulip. Some of special beauty for growing and cutting are:

PARROT TULIPS

These flower in April and May and have fantastic feathery flowers with twisted petals. The large flowers are useful for arrangement in the manner of Flemish and Dutch flower paintings.

Black parrot (dark purple)	Orange parrot
Blue parrot (mauve-blue)	Red parrot
Fantasy (pink)	White parrot
Fire Bird (red)	Sunshine (yellow)

TULIPA VIRIDIFLORA

These flower in April and early May and are medium sized flowers. They are an old group made popular again by flower arrangers and have very lovely colours laced with green.

Artist – apricot	Golden Artist (new expensive now) – yellow
Greenland – cream and pink	Pimpernel – rose
Hollywood – red	Doorman – raspberry red
Angel – white	Viridiflora – green

FRINGED TULIPS

Those flowers have finely fringed petals, the bulbs are still rather expensive.
Burgundy Lace
Fringed Flamingo
Swan Wings
Picture

REMBRANDT

This tulip flowers in May and is perfect for the 'flower painting' style of flower arrangements as they are stripey.

Absalon	mahogany flashes on yellow
Insulinde	bronze, purple and brown on yellow
Black Boy	golden feathers on brown
Pierette	lilac and lavendar on silver-cream
Sorbet	white splashed pink

DOUBLE EARLY TULIPS

The flower appears in April–May, with short stems and double petals.

Bonanza	orange	Marechal Niel	yellow
Electra	pink-mauve	Mount Tacoma	white
Mermione	pink-white	Schoonoord	white
Lilac Perfection	deep pink		

'Pride of Holland' is especially beautiful being like a big crimson peony.

DARWIN TULIPS AND DARWIN HYBRIDS

Flowering in May, these are tall and have some of the largest flowers.

Black Swan	maroon
Lavendar Lady	two shades of light mauve
La Tulipe Noire	almost black
Queen of Knight	dark red
Sweet Harmony	yellow, white edge
Gudoshnik	brilliant red and yellow

COTTAGE TULIPS

Late April and early May is the flowering time.

Blushing Bride	yellow with pink edge
Bond St	yellow streaked with orange
Dillenburg	orange streaked with yellow
Mothers Day	red and yellow

LILY FLOWERING

These flower in April. They are not the water-lily variety which in shorter and called *T. kaufmanniana*.

Astor	bronze tinged pink
Clarice	clear yellow
Queen of Sheba	brown-orange edged light orange
White Triumphator	

OTHERS

T. whitalli, small brown-orange tulip
Multi-flowered, several smaller flowers clustered on a stem – Orange Bouquet, Rosy Mist.

Hyacinth

The sweet smelling hyacinth grows wild in Greece but has been cultivated to produce a much larger and more compact flower. As a cut flower they can be difficult because of their heavy heads, often out of proportion with the stem but they are irresistible for their beauty and perfume. The Roman hyacinth is a useful group for flower arrangement growing two to three to a bulb and with looser, less compact heads.

Buying Bulbs

Buy those with lighter flower heads rather than 'Extra Choice' which are very heavy. 15/16 cms are smaller flowered than those of 17/18 cms.

The Site

Nothing can be more beautiful than a bed entirely of hyacinth but it is rather expensive. As they are low growing, hyacinth are successful grown under other plants such as roses. I have seen them looking very lovely growing in grass under a fruit tree. A light or semi-shaded position is suitable.

Planting

WHEN TO PLANT

Plant in October or November.

HOW TO PLANT

Plant about 5"–6" deep and 6" apart, covering with 4" of soil. Rake in a handful of bonemeal per square yard at planting time. If the soil is heavy work in some peat and sand as they do better in a light soil.

Lifting

Lift in July when the foliage dies down or earlier to a temporary place if the bed is wanted. However they will come up again if left. If lifted, dry off and place in a cool, dry place after shaking

69

away the soil, twisting off the withered leaves and roots. Replant in October, retaining only the larger bulbs.

Hyacinth for Growing and Arranging

Chestnut Flower	double pale pink
City of Haarlem	yellow
Fairy Blue	pale blue
Lady Derby	soft pink
Perle Brilliant	blue
Queen of the Whites	
Rosalie	deep rose pink
Yellow Hammer	cream

H. orientalis albulus (Roman Hyacinth) in white, pink and blue.

Alliums

The ornamental relations of the onions are exciting flowers and seedheads to use for flower arrangements especially in modern

Allium rosenbachianum, *seedhead*

designs, as they have flowers which are quite round. Some are small and others as big as footballs.

Site

The site should be open in full sun with a well drained soil. Alliums may be planted in groups between low-growing shrubs or perennials.

Planting

WHEN TO PLANT

Plant in September–October.

HOW TO PLANT

Plant three or four in a group for the best effect at a depth of 6″–18″ according to the size of the flower.

Lifting

This is unnecessary as alliums grow better when untouched for several years. If the clumps become very thick and the flowers are poor they should be divided and replanted at once in the Autumn.

Deadheading

It unlikely that this will be necessary in a flower arranger's garden as the seedheads dry well for winter use. If possible cut only short stems to avoid starving the bulbs.

For Growing and Arranging

Allium albopilosum Height 18″, 6″ flower umbels in June of pale purple. 4″–5″ apart. Useful seedheads for drying.
A. aflatunense Height 30″, planting distance 9″, 3″–4″ umbels in May–June of rosy-purple. Good seedheads.
A. giganteum Height 48″, planting distance 9″–12″ apart, greyish-blue flowers in June, glaucous foliage 4″ or more umbels. Good to dry.
A. porrum (leek) biennial, exciting stems which may twist.

A. siculum   Height 2′–4′, planting distance 9″. Exciting bell-shaped flowers in green, white and chestnut in May-June. The flower is in a cluster rather than an umbel.

A. rosenbachianum   Height 30″ planting distance 6″–9″, umbels in May–June of purple flowers 5″–6″ in size.

A. schoenoprasum sibiricum (giant chives)   Scabious-like flowers in pink-mauve, useful for flavouring also. It should be cut to the ground as the flowers fade and a second crop will appear.

A. schoenoprasum (chives)   Height 6″–10″, planting distance 12″ rose-pink flowers 1″ across in June and July. May be grown indoors in pots for winter use. Lift in October for this. It grows well in window-boxes in John Innes No. 1. It should be divided every four years.

Iris

The story of the iris began centuries ago and a Pharaoh of Egypt is thought to have brought back an iris from his Syrian wars in 1950 B.C. – it is carved on a marble panel on the temple of Theban Ammon at Karnak. Often represented in Japanese art, and the flower which was the Royal Emblem of France, it has been loved by many poets. There are many varieties from many habitats and they include Bearded, Beardless, Crested and Bulbous sections. This chapter is concerned with the bulbous flowers, *I. xiphium* hybrids called Dutch, Spanish and English Iris. Plant them in September or October 4″–6″ deep with a planting distance of 6″–8″.

Dutch Irises

These are the first to flower from June–July. The height is 15″–24″ and they should be planted 4″–6″ apart. The colours include white, yellow, blue, bronze and purple. They thrive in a light fertile soil in full sun. Winter protection will be needed in many parts of Britain. Those growing in wet and heavy soils should be lifted in late summer and stored until planting time in September or October.

Good plants are:

Wedgwood	light blue
Angels Wings	yellow and white
Bronze Queen	copper bronze

| Orange King | orange |
| Lemon Queen | two shades of yellow |

Spanish Iris

These flower a little later than the Dutch iris, and the flower is smaller. There is a good range of colours including smoky shades. They require a light soil and a warmer and drier position than the Dutch Iris. They should be lifted when the foliage has died down.

| Hercules | bronze, gold and blue |
| Gipsy Girl | purple, grey and amber |

English

The easiest to cultivate, they thrive in a rich damp soil and become well established as a perennial. They do not require lifting and should not be left out of the ground for long as the bulbs deteriorate. The colours are more limited – white, blue, purple and mauve but no yellows. These may be brought in mixed collections.

| Mont Blanc | white |
| King of the Blues | dark blue |

Mention should be made here of the charming Little Widow Iris, La Vedovina in Italian Gardens, which is *Hermodactylus tuberosus* described once as made of 'black velvet and dull green silk'. It is very small and hardy in warm situations but can take a year to become established.

Iris foetidissima Is another favourite of flower arrangers for its scarlet seeds in Autumn which dry well. It is a rhizome, height 20″, planting distance 12″–18″ with evergreen foliage. The flowers are poor. There is a variegated form and both have the orange seedheads. It should be planted in Autumn in *moist*, rich soils $1\frac{1}{2}$″ deep. It may take a year to settle down and flower. It can be increased by dividing.

Spring Bulbs in Pots

Bulbs are specially prepared and may be bought for forcing in bowls from late August–October to flower in mid-December and onwards. Hyacinth, early single and double tulips, narcissi and daffodils are all successful and make lovely Christmas presents.

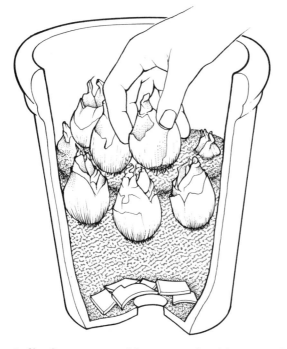

Bulbs from a reputable source should be bought as the preparation must be carefully carried out including correct lifting, drying and storing at the correct temperature.

METHOD

1 The bulbs should be grown in John Innes No. 2 potting compost or in a bulb fibre sold for this purpose. Those placed in J.I.2 usually flower the following year when placed in the garden afterwards but those grown in fibre (which is cleaner to use) may not flower until a year later in the garden.

2 Moisten the compost or fibre and place a layer in a pot (it need not have holes in the bottom).

3 Stand the bulbs on this and add more compost or fibre. The bulbs can touch each other and in the case of daffodils two layers can be placed in a deep pot.

4 Cover all bulbs with compost or fibre with the exception of large hyacinth or daffodils. The surface of the medium should be below the top of the pot to allow for watering.

5 Place the bowls in a cool place to root, about eight to ten weeks. The bowls may be stood out of doors in a box and covered

with peat or ashes. A place such as a shelf in a dark coal shed is also suitable.

6 Water every two or three weeks if the pots seem dry.

7 When the tips of the leaves are showing 1"–2" move the bowls into a cool room in the light and to get used to warmth gradually. The best temperature is 50°F.

8 When the leaves are 4" high they can go into a warmer room. Bowls can be brought in gradually for a succession of flowers and the bulbs are not harmed if this is delayed even if the leaves are showing.

9 When the flowers are over, cut them off, but not the stems or leaves. Move the bowls back to a light cool place and keep watering. In March or April place the whole clump in the garden. They will flower out-of-doors next season but are not suitable for forcing again.

CALENDAR

August–September	Plant daffodils
August–October	Plant bulbs in pots for forcing
September–October	Plant alliums and irises
October–November	Plant hyacinths and tulips

Narcissus 'King Alfred' grown in a pot

Arranging the Flowers

The flowers of Spring bulbous plants are really delightful to arrange. Their fragile beauty and clear colours are so refreshing after weeks of arranging the heavier-looking chrysanthemums, evergreens and dried and preserved plant material. Their crisp, clean appearance seems so right for the beginning of the year and their colourings are cheerful when the days are still cold.

Cutting

Cut stems as short as possible and only cut a few leaves as these, if left on the bulb, help to store it with food to make next year's flowers. The flowers do not need to go into a bucket of water carried into the garden as the stems easily take up water. They are adapted to pierce hard, cold soil and as a result do not wilt easily. Cut in bud as open Spring flowers do not last long in the house. Their petals are used to cool temperatures and the house is often kept very warm and dry in winter.

Conditioning

No special preparation of the stems is needed and these flowers may be arranged at once. It is possible for the stems to become soggy if soaked in deep water for long periods and they are better arranged, as all bulbous flowers, in shallow water. The stem end sometimes has a white section and this should be cut off as it sometimes does not take up water well.

WILTING This is rare as the stems are sturdy and even when a daffodil flower is dead its stem is usually standing up straight like a sentinel. Some stems of bought iris can be weak but this is usually because of forcing in heat and does not apply to the garden iris. Tulips have notorious stems which, as the flower matures, swing around in different directions when the cut stem is placed in water. Flower arrangers have tried various stiffening practices which are meant to keep the stems in the required position. They may stay put for a day or two but, sure enough, as the flower matures the stem will start to bend. Some people, determined to make them stay put, do wire them. It seems a pity not to enjoy the lovely curves which usually result from the gyrations and if really not to your liking it is a simple matter to reposition a stem in the container. The flowers of daffodils and iris do not last as long as those of tulips, hyacinths and alliums.

Transporting

Spring flowers are easier to transport in tight bud and will soon come out when placed in warm water. This is especially true of iris flowers and daffodils as their intricate shapes are not easy to pack and are easily crushed.

Mechanics

Pinholders are ideal for all the stems with the exception of iris which are sometimes too slender to go on the pins. These can be placed in a section of hollow stem and then placed on the pinholder. Alternatively a short piece of twig can be used as a splint at the base of the stem, held on with a short length of reel wire. Spring flower stems also go into wire netting but may become soggy in the deep water that goes with netting. They are very successful in Oasis with the exception of over-soaked daffodils with soft stems.

WIRING HYACINTH

I feel that the wiring of cut flower stems should be done as little as possible as the result is often an unnatural, stiff and contrived appearance. Hyacinth are however an exception. The flower heads have been developed out of proportion with their soft stems and they often flop with the weight out-of-doors and certainly in arrangements. The stem gives way as it is pushed into Oasis or on to a pinholder. But it is a pity not to use them because of this. A stub wire, a stiff short wire from the florist, can be inserted into the stem end and guided up the stem until it comes near the top. Bend the top of the wire around the stem amongst the flowers and cut off the bottom end leaving about $1\frac{1}{2}''$ of wire sticking out. Push this into the Oasis so that it supports the flower. The stem end of the hyacinth must also go into the Oasis to get water.

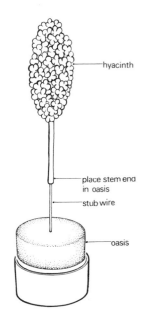

hyacinth

place stem end
in oasis

stub wire

oasis

Preserving

The narcissus family dries well in a desiccant. Cut off most of the
stem and push a stub wire through the top of the remaining stem.
This can be bent over in the desiccant while the flower is drying
which takes about three days in silica gel.

Alliums dry beautifully in the air if it is not damp. The large
round seedheads may crush each other and they are best hung
separately, or placed on pinholders.

Narcissi press well for pressed flower pictures, especially in
a flower press. The short cupped varieties can be pressed flat
if you squash the cup firmly down with your thumb when
placing the flower on the blotting paper. Daffodils with long
trumpets cannot be pressed so easily and should be dissected
with nail scissors. Cut the trumpet from the petals and then cut
it again in half lengthwise. Press the petals flat – these may also
be cut for pressing. Re-assemble the parts when glueing them
on to the background. Two flowers seen sideways will result
from pressing one daffodil.

Design

Most Spring flowers and especially daffodils and irises look
their best in simple designs and appear very beautiful combined
with wood and bare branches.

Narcissi

The straight stems are not suitable for designs where curves are
wanted and many flower arrangers enjoy them arranged as they
grow – vertically in a small grouping. The stems of buds are
normally shorter in length than the open flowers but this looks
quite natural when they are arranged. The flowers need to be

turned to face different directions so that the lovely shape can be seen from all angles.

STYLES One of the loveliest ways to arrange daffodils and narcissi is on a pinholder in a food tin (the shallow water is quite sufficient) placed on a slate base or crosscut of wood. A Honister stone base is very suitable as daffodils are often seen growing in the Lake District against this stone. A bare winter branch or two can be used with them and perhaps a little foliage from *elaeagnus pungens maculata* or aucuba, both of which are green and gold. Moss, stones, or a small chunk of driftwood can hide the food tin. This is called a landscape design.

Narcissi are also effective placed on a pinholder in a food tin plunged into a grouping of pot plants and this is called a pot-et-fleur. They are lovely too in baskets.

The narcissi with short cups are very eye-catching and it is necessary to turn them in all directions as they do rather 'stare' out otherwise. Two or three look excellent as a centre of interest in a design of other plant material.

Iris

These lovely flowers have not such eye-pull as rounded flowers and their shape is delicate and intricate. For this reason they need to be arranged simply with a gentle touch. They are effective combined with bulrushes and ferns, in a design which features water. They also look lovely in glass which suits their fragility and the pinholder can be concealed with shattered windscreen glass. I cringe when I see iris flower heads chopped off with short stems as, when placed low in a design, it is impossible to see their delicate shape. They look their best when seen clearly in space on the top of tall stems. Normally they look better arranged without other flowers but with the foliage of other plants, such as fern and arum, or small aspidistra.

Tulips

These are good mixers but also excellent flowers on their own and are more versatile than iris and daffodils. Their clean beauty is especially suitable for table arrangements and their strong shape makes them right for modern designs. The slender tapering buds are suitable for the extremities, the half open flowers for 'stepping stones' and open flowers for the centre of the design. The foliage is also excellent. It should be used on a short length of stem. Mature flowers can be pressed open by placing the thumb underneath the centre of each petal and turning the petal back with the first two fingers. This can make a fabulous focal point if the tulip is a large and exotic one. The Rembrandt tulips are especially desirable in mixed groupings of flowers in the manner of a Flemish or Dutch flower painting.

Much of the early foliage of Spring looks lovely with tulips such as the maple 'Brilliantissimum' which is apricot coloured in the Spring, the whitebeam with its almost white foliage, and young sycamore which is light red and brown. Bought carnations are effective as the roughness of these combines well with the silky smoothness of the tulips, and *euphorbia polychroma* provides another 'rough-looking' yellow flower for contrast.

Hyacinth

These can be arranged alone in a bowl with wire netting for the support and are very beautiful. They are also good with tulips as they provide a 'pattern' in contrast with the smooth tulip flower. They have short stems so must be used low in a design but are always desirable because of their perfume.

Alliums

These 'balls' of flowers are excellent for modern arrangements and two or three can be enough in a design combined with driftwood or dramatic foliage. They do have an onion smell but this can be avoided if a teaspoonful of Milton or similar disinfectant is used to a pint of water in the container. The stem ends should not be placed in boiling water as this increases the onion smell.

Containers

Hidden containers are suitable for Spring flowers which do not need deep water. Glass suits their type of beauty as does basketry and wood. Heavy, large, metal and stoneware containers are not so successful except with the bigger more dramatic tulips as Spring flowers are smaller in size than many Summer and Autumn flowers and need containers with less visual weight.

4 Hardy Perennials

The herbaceous perennial is soft in growth as distinct from a tree or shrub which has a woody stem and it can live for any number of years. Most perennials die down to the ground each winter. There are hardy, half-hardy and tender perennials but this is often dependent on the climate. The most useful group are the *hardy* perennials which can be grown out-of-doors in most parts of the British Isles, without protection.

Perennials provide a great variety of cut flowers and include all the lovely plants associated with a British garden in summer – peonies, delphiniums, poppies and so on. Many are useful for their leaves or seedheads which can be dried or treated with glycerine. Their great advantage in the garden is their long life as they do not have to be renewed annually as bedding plants. Their disadvantage is that they die down in the Autumn and can look rather untidy through the winter but it is exciting to watch them pusing through the earth again in Spring with their strong shoots. Perennials grow quickly and are easily increased so neighbours and friends are often willing to share plants. A few are evergreen and there are some which flower during winter.

Growing Perennials

Choosing Plants

In my early days of gardening and flower arranging I bought many plants through catalogues. I was quite carried away with the growing descriptions but some of the plants turned out to be a complete waste of money. I waited anxiously for them to flower only to find I did not like the colour, shape or size or that the flower did not condition well for flower arrangement. There is no substitute for actually seeing the plant in flower. There are many gardens open to the public with borders and beds of hardy perennials and if you visit those near your home you will be more likely to see plants which will suit the local climate and thrive in your own garden. The plants are normally labelled so take a pad and pen for writing down the Latin names. This is essential when ordering as popular names are not consistent. Visiting flower shows, nurseries and garden centres can provide a pleasant weekend afternoon occupation and the names of good plants can be collected on the visit. At Flower Clubs demonstrators of flower arrangement normally

Curtonus paniculatus *provides useful leaves*

give the names of the plants they use and this is especially useful to the flower arranging gardener. Catalogues and horticultural books are certainly useful but not a complete substitute for seeing the plant in flower.

Some suppliers have collections of perennials for flower arrangers and these are useful for people in a hurry to have flowers for cutting, but the mixed border collections which are well selected for height, colour and a continuing flowering season, do not necessarily provide good plants for cutting.

The disadvantage of not being sure that a plant is useful for garden and home is that money, space and time are wasted. It also seems slightly sinful to dig up and throw out a plant which is thriving simply because the colour of the flower does not look well in your home. However take courage and heave out your mistakes as they only take up precious space. It is important to get plants which are really useful into the ground quickly as they may take time to become sufficiently established to produce enough flowers for cutting.

After two or three years you will find out the plants which thrive in the conditions you have in your garden. These are the ones on which to concentrate and increase if you have little time for gardening. The other sickly ones will need too much attention and it is sensible to get rid of them if they never do anything. Once I decide that a plant is useful for flower arranging and easy to grow then I buy several more plants or, if the original one is big enough, I divide it to give more plants and in this way there can be many of the flowers you like to cut. This is more useful than having many different varieties with only a few flowers on each.

The Site

An open sunny position is better although a few plants will grow in light shade. The herbaceous border of perennials, after years of popularity, is now going out of fashion in favour of island beds. These may be of any size and for the smaller garden 9' × 3' would be suitable. Alternatively many people mix roses, shrubs and perennials together most successfully. The artistic background to a herbaceous border provided by a hedge or high wall is not always a help when growing the plants. My own beech hedge caused all the plants to lean away and also to grow too leggy in their search for more light. I am happier with an island bed nearer the centre of the lawn. Plants in free-standing beds are less likely to need staking than those in borders as they do not grow so tall and this is work-saving.

Perennials benefit from lifting, dividing and replanting about every third year and this can be an opportunity to try a free-standing bed perhaps in the shape of a crescent, boomerang or

An island bed

kidney. The plant may well take on a new lease of life and the old bed can be turfed over with the grass removed from the new site.

Planting

WHEN TO PLANT

The best months for planting are October when perennials are beginning to slow down growth and March and April when they are beginning growth again. Container-grown perennials can be planted at any time as long as the soil is not frozen or water-logged which is unpleasant weather for man and plant! The nursery men are a great help and usually send the plants at the most safe and suitable time for transplanting. Some thrive better planted in the Spring and others need Autumn planting. Spring planting is better on heavy, clay soils.

If plants are delivered when the soil cannot be dug then cover them with wet sacking or newspaper and keep them in a frost free garage or shed, planting out as soon as possible.

SOIL PREPARATION

Dig over a new bed and include garden compost, mushroom compost, hop manure or animal manure at the rate of one bucketful to a square yard or a good barrowful to six square yards. Remove all weeds and do this meticulously to save later work. Leave the ground to settle down for a week or two and then just before planting scatter about one handful of bonemeal over each square yard of bed and rake the soil over.

HOW TO PLANT

Dig a hole the same shape as the roots and big enough to take them without squashing up. The depth of planting can be estimated by the level of the old soil showing on the plants but if this is not apparent, make sure the top roots are covered by at least an inch of soil.

If the ground is very dry pour water into the hole and let it drain down before placing the plant in the hole. This is called puddling in (lovely expression). Make sure the soil is very firm around the roots by treading the soil down.

SPACING

Plants should be spaced about 2' apart if they are tall (the catalogues indicate the eventual height), 1' apart if medium sized (about 3' high, when grown) and 6" apart if small (about 1' high). I tend to err on the close side as I like a mass of plants with little soil between each one. In herbaceous borders the tallest plants are placed at the back but they are usually in the centre, or to one side of the centre, in an island bed.

Puddling in a hardy perennial

Treading down soil around a plant

Mulching

Mulch at the beginning of May with 1"-2" of peat, preferably over the whole bed. The peat should be moist.

Staking

Some perennials need support especially if you live in a windy district, but the very tall (over 4') plants are not a lot of use for flower arrangement – for example, smaller delphiniums are much more suitable for the house than those 6' tall – and the smaller plants stand up alone which saves work in staking. Plants in island beds may not need staking as they are often less leggy. If staking is necessary there are these methods:

1 Place canes well into the ground and tie separate stems to each cane. This is suitable for delphiniums. Do not tie very tightly to avoid cutting the stem.
2 Thrust short bushy branches around each plant when it is a few inches high and it will grow through the branches and be supported.
3 Buy special wire supports made for staking plants.

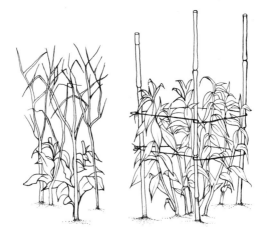

supporting perennials

Feeding

A good general fertilizer applied at the rate of a large handful to each square yard of bed in February or March will be adequate for the needs of established plants.

frequent hoeing kills seedling weeds

Weeds

Unfortunately there is no weed-killer which can choose between a lovely peony or poppy and a weed and it will kill both if carelessly applied. Very exact application is necessary if a weed-killer is used on a bed of perennials and I think it is too difficult, having lost several plants this way. The dying weeds also look unattractive amongst the plants. Hoeing and hand weeding is better and a good mulch will help to prevent many weeds.

Dividing

A perennial normally grows very quickly and the centre part becomes worn out. The plant will continue to grow well if it is divided up, which simply means that the original large root is split into several pieces all of which are separately planted. This is an easy method of propagating (increasing) perennials. Lift the plant from the bed with a fork. It can then be divided by these methods:

1 If the plant is small break off pieces with the hand.
2 If the plant is large thrust two forks back to back well into the centre. Lever the handles apart and the plant should neatly divide into two. This can be done more than once with a big plant.
3 If the plant has a very hard centre it may need to be cut with a knife but do this carefully to avoid damaging the roots.

Each new plant should have remaining some good roots and several growing shoots. The worn-out central portion can be thrown away.

The best months for dividing are March and April just before the plant starts to grow strongly. Perennials can also be grown from seed or from stem or root cuttings but the busy person is usually happy with dividing to increase stock and to keep the plant growing well.

General Care

Cut off dead growth in Autumn to neaten the appearance of the plant. In cold districts some of this may be left on through the winter to give protection but it can be unsightly.

Calendar

October	Plant
	Tidy up beds
March	Plant
	Divide plants
	Feed
May	Stake
	Mulch

(top) Breaking a plant to divide it
(left) Dividing with two forks
(right) Cutting with a knife

Arranging Perennials

The variety of flower, foliage and seedhead provided through this group of plants is very great and the art of the flower arranger can be really explored. There are endless combinations of plants to try, many different shapes, an infinite number of colours and textures and various styles. The summer is the time for trying the innumerable possibilities. It is also a time for mass designs and huge pedestal arrangements of flowing abundance. In the winter starker designs using more space, fewer flowers, preserved plant material and driftwood are more appropriate but in the summer the house can be a riot of colour using flowers cut from the garden with little or no expense.

Cutting

Perennials can be cut at any time of the day but in hot or very dry weather it is better to cut in the early morning or late evening when the plant contains more water. During the hot part of the day the plant will be transpiring rapidly and contain less water which means it is more likely to wilt when cut.

Select flowers to cut which are not fully open as these will last longer in the house and cut the stem close to the base of the plant. Place the stems in a bucket half-full of tepid water, if possible taken into the garden. If this is not done then recut the stem end before placing it in water, as many plants when exposed to the air grow a seal over the end and this prevents water from entering. Cutting removes the seal.

Conditioning

If you take a bucket half-full of tepid water into the garden to collect the flowers as you cut, fill it up to the top in the house. Water can move into a stem through the outside tissue when the stems are in deep water. Leave the stems to soak for about two hours to prepare them for the heat and dryness of the house, preferably in a cool, dim place as this stops the flowers from developing too quickly.

STEMS

The stems of perennials may be hard or soft but few are really woody. Soft stems need no more than soaking but the harder stems should have a cut made vertically up the stem for an inch as this exposes more of the inner tissue to water. Some stems contain latex which leaks out when a flower is cut – poppies and euphorbias are examples. This leakage can be stopped by holding the stem-end in the flame of a match or gas-jet. There will be a sizzling noise and when this stops and the stem end is

A triangular design of perennials including Achillea filipendulina *'Gold Plate'*, Kniphofia tubergenii *(a yellow red-hot poker)*, Alchemilla mollis

All the hostas are useful for flower arrangement

blackened, place the flower back in the bucket. If the stem is cut again when making the arrangement it should be re-singed.

FOLIAGE

The leaves of perennials can take in water through their surface and conditioning is easy if they are pushed under water in a bowl or sink for about two hours. Young foliage soon wilts and until after May leaves may be difficult to condition. Until this time pick the oldest leaves you can find as they are more likely to 'stand up'.

Grey leaves should not be submerged as the small hairs which give the grey effect become waterlogged and continue to drip all over the furniture after their removal from the water. The greyness is also lost.

WILTING

Wilting flowers can be revived by:

1 Removing the flower from the arrangement, recutting the stem-end and placing the stem in deep warm water for an hour or two.

2 Floating the flower in water for about an hour.
3 Recutting the stem end and placing it in an inch of very hot water. Leave until the water is cool and then replace the revived flower in the arrangement.
4 Submerging under cold water, which is sometimes helpful but an hour is long enough as delicate flower tissues soon become damaged.

Mechanics

The stems of perennials are normally hard enough for any of the standard methods of support. Sometimes, when young, the stems are too soft for plastic foam and a pinholder or wire netting is easier. Cutting a soft stem to a point before pushing it into the foam is helpful.

Oasis in an ash-tray being covered with Tellima *leaves and small flowers for a table centrepiece*

The candle is pushed through the Oasis before being placed in the candlestick

Dried delphiniums with glycerined foliage and fresh single chrysanthemums, arranged by Molly Duerr

Peonies and leaves floating with shells for a summer table centrepiece

Iris with Spring foliage of whitebeam, to lighten a dark hall. Arranged by Dorothy Haworth

Foliage of *Mahonia* 'Charity' and *M. bealei*, holly of the variety
'Golden King', trails of *Euonymus fortunei* 'Variegata' with hydrangea
flowers and peacocks' feathers for an economical Autumn
arrangement.

Preserving

Many perennials can be dried or preserved with glycerine and this is stated with the plant descriptions which follow. Small flowers and leaves which are fairly flat can be pressed for flower pictures.

Design

There is no limit to the designs which can be made with perennial flowers, leaves, seedheads and even stems. Whatever the style space, even if minimal, should be left around each flower so that it can be seen well; flowers should be turned to face different ways as all parts of a flower are beautiful; the stems should be cut to different lengths so that the flowers are seen clearly at different levels.

SCALE

When mixing different varieties together be sure that they are related in size with each other and with the container. Huge flowers such as the biggest dahlias look odd with small leaves and vice-versa.

COLOUR

Any colours can be combined together and there are no rules. The main thing is that the flower arrangement should suit the room in which it is placed and that you enjoy the colours you have placed together. Usually it is better to keep to a colour 'key' and use either all soft, subtle colours together, all brilliant ones or all pale ones. If one colour seems to stand out and hit you then it is probably better to remove it. White can be difficult as it is very eye catching and is usually better when combined with pale colours or used in an all white arrangement.

One spot of a colour often seems difficult to incorporate into a design and colours look better if there is more than one of each – in other words if colours are repeated.

Variety in colouring brings more life and interest and an arrangement of only two colours – say a yellow and a green can be dull but easily improved by the use of several greens. One day try collecting all the greens you can from the garden and you may be surprised at the number of different ones and how lovely they look together and the same applies to other colours.

COMBINING PLANT MATERIAL

Sometimes one variety of flower, such as delphinium, looks lovely arranged on its own and this really seems to emphasize its special beauty. The addition of leaves from another plant may be necessary to conceal the mechanics. At other times you may enjoy combining different shapes and a pleasing design can be made by cutting some long flowers such as delphiniums, some rounded flowers such as peonies and some rather oval shaped leaves such as those of the hosta. These three different shapes combine well together and are a good basic recipe for combining the shapes of plant material.

The Dutch and Flemish flower paintings show many shapes and colours together and this style is a lovely one for the summer months when there is plenty of variety in the garden. Buy a postcard of such a painting to study the way the flowers are combined and placed.

There are very many perennial plants which are attractive both as growing plants in the garden and for cut flowers, leaves and seedheads in the house. The following is a basic collection, but improvements are being continuously made and new varieties added to catalogues. All are hardy in most of the British Isles and easy to grow. Some are useful for flowers and foliage, some preserve or dry well and this is stated. They are plants which I find useful and I wish I had found a similar list when I started flower arrangement as it might have eliminated a lot of trial and error.

Achillea (yarrow) *A. filipendulina* 'Gold Plate' 4', July/August. This dries very well when hung upside down. It is visually rough in appearance and invaluable for use in dried arrangements. This is a good yellow but there are also white, lemon and carmine varieties.

Alchemilla mollis (lady's mantle) 12"–18", June/August. Small brilliant yellow/green flowers which combine well with many other flowers. The small rounded leaves are excellent for hiding mechanics. In the garden it makes good ground cover. Glycerines.

Anaphalis (pearl everlasting) *A. yedoensis*, up to 24", July/
September. The small grey-white flowers dry well when hung
up.

Anthemis tinctoria (Golden Marguerite) 'E.C. Buxton', lemon-
yellow and 'Grallagh Gold', deep yellow. The flower presses
well and keeps its colour better than any other. 2½', June/
August.

Arum italicum (a form of Lords and Ladies). 'Pictum' gives excellent winter foliage. The leaves are dark green veined with
light green. It needs plenty of a general fertilizer for big leaves.
The short stems are better on a pinholder. The leaves can be
picked under the snow.

Astilbe 'Peach Blossom', pale pink. 'Gloria', white.

Astrantia (masterwort) *A. major* 24", July/August. Charming,
small Victorian looking flower. They last well in water and
have a subtle colour. Press and dry.

Ballota pseudo-dictamnus 12"–24" woolly-grey leaves in whorls.

Bergenia (elephant's ear). All varieties are useful for foilage to
cover mechanics. They make useful ground cover and are
evergreen. *B. cordifolia* has round leaves, *B. crassifolia* has
ovate leaves, *B. purpurascens* colours well in Autumn. The
flower can be useful. The leaves take glycerine but need mop-
ping as well as standing in the mixture.

Campanula (bellflower) *C. lactiflora* 4', June/July. 'Loddon
Anna', pink, 'Pouffe', lavender. Press individual flowers.

Centaurea macrocephala (perennial cornflower) 3'–5', June/July.
Long lasting yellow flowers, good for modern designs.

Chrysanthemum maximum (shasta daisy) 3', July/August. 'Wirral
Supreme' double white. Lasts well in water.

Curtonus paniculatus. A cormous plant, 4', August. Giant mont-
bretia seedheads dry, leaves press well.

Cynara cardunculus (cardoon) 5'. Greyish green, graceful large,
long leaves, suitable for pedestal arrangements. Mulch well
in cold places before the winter. Heads dry well by hanging up.

Delphinium elatum, the Dwarf varieties which grow to about 4',
are the most suitable for flower arrangement as they are not
too tall, and are more branched. The shorter branches are very
useful. 'Lord Butler' pale blue, 'Bonita' gentian blue, 'Moer-
heimii' white, 'Blue Jade' pale blue, brown eyes, 'Pink Sen-
sation' pink and there are others. June/July. Hang up to dry.

Dianthus (pink) *Dx allwoodii* are the modern pink, May/August.

Eryngium alpinium *which takes glycerine well*

Doronicum (leopard's bane) *D. plantagineum* 'Harpur Crewe' has golden yellow flowers, 24″, April/June. Press, silica gel.

Echinacea (purple cone flower) 3′, July/September. *E. purpurea* 'Robert Bloom' is purple rose.

Echinops (globe thistle) *E. ritro* globular, steel-blue flowers, 4′, July/August. The flowers dry if picked before they come out.

Eryngium (sea-holly) *E. alpinum* 18″–24″, fluffy blue, grey or mauve bracts, short-lived plant but glycerines. *E. giganteum* (Miss Willmott's ghost) is monocarpic and dies after flowering 4′, dries well. *E. variifolium* 2′ has marbled white leaves, ever-green. All July/September flowers. Dry by hanging up.

Euphorbia (spurge) *E. polychroma* 18″, April/May. Long lasting, long flowering with bright yellow flowers and bracts. *E. robbiae*, rosette shaped foliage is useful for covering mechanics 18″, thrives in shade. *E. griffithii* has red bracts 'Fireglow' is a good variety 2½′, May/June. *E. palustris* is like *E. polychroma* but larger and June/July. *E. sikkimensis* bright red young growth, yellow bracts July/August. *E. pilosa* 'Major' is like *E. polychroma* but larger. Wash the hands well after using euphorbias as some people are allergic to the juice in the stem. Burn the stem end to prevent leakage.

Foeniculum vulgare (common fennel) 6', lacy dainty yellow flowers. Remove the flowers the first year to make it a perennial. Can seed itself May/June. Press.

Filipendula purpurea 2½' deep rose, dainty flowers, likes shade.

Gaillardia aristata 2½' June/October 'Mandarin' is a flame-orange variety, daisy-like.

Helenium autumnale 4'-6', August/October. Many yellow to crimson varieties, last well in water. Dry in silica gel.

Helianthus (sunflower) *H. decapetalus* 'Soleil d'Or' 4'-6', August/September, silica gel.

Helleborus (Christmas and Lenten roses) *H. niger* 'Potters Wheel' 12", January/March, white flowers. *H. foetidus* 24", March/May, yellow green flowers. *H. argutifolius* (Corsican hellebore) evergreen leaves take glycerine well, March/April, yellow-green flowers. All the hellebores are lovely in the garden because they are winter and early Spring flowers but not all

Helleborus argutifolius, *syn.* H. corsicus, *an evergreen perennial*

hold up well in the house until they are in the seed stage. Press or dry in silica gel.

Hemerocallis (day-lily) 3', July/August. A wide range of colours including delicate pinks and apricots. Although each flower lasts only a short time a stem can be used in arrangement and dead flowers removed leaving buds to come out.

Hosta (plantain lily) all varieties are invaluable for their foliage in arrangements. They make excellent ground cover. A selection are *H. fortunei* 'Aureo-marginata has a yellow margin, 'Albopicta' is pale green and yellow variegated. *H. sieboldiana* – big blue-green leaves. *H. lancifolia* – long, small leaves. *H. crispula* has white margins. *H. undulata* – wavy leaves. *H. tokudama* has glaucous in-curved leaves, there is also a variegated form. The leaves will sometimes take glycerine.

Iris (germanica bearded or flag iris). These grow from rhizomes. The leaves are invaluable for flower arrangements and the flowers are dramatic in simple designs. There are many colours. $2\frac{1}{2}'-5'$, May/June. Plant in late June preferably with the rhizomes just showing in full sun. Press leaves.

Kniphofia (red hot poker) June/October, with a selection which flowers at different times. Heights from $1\frac{1}{2}'-5'$. White and yellow to red.

Lobelia cardinalis $2\frac{1}{2}'$, July/August, brilliant red flowers with dark leaves. Short lived and need shelter.

Lychnis chalcedonica (Maltese cross) 2'–3', July/August, scarlet heads.

Macleaya cordata (plume poppy) 5'–8' tall stems with small white flowers, decorative leaves with grey underside will press. *M. microcarpa* 'Coral Plume' has brown-pink flowers.

Meconopsis grandis 24", May/June, brilliant blue poppy-like flower not long-lasting when cut but unusual colour. Press.

Myosotis alpestris (forget-me-not) 6", April/June. Press small blue flowers.

Nepeta (catmint) *N.x. faassenii* 12"–18", May/September, small blue flowers.

Paeonia (peony) 3' May, many lovely colours. Leaves glycerine. Flowers silica gel. Very beautiful tree peonies are 'Souvenir de Maxime Cornu', 'Chromatella', 'Lord Selbourne'.

Papaver orientale (Oriental poppy) 3', May/June. Better cut as a bud barely showing colour. Singe the stem-end. Dry seed-heads.

Phlox paniculata 3', July/September. Many colours.

Phormium tenax (New Zealand flax). Needs shelter, grown for iris-like leaves. 'Purpureum' is dark red, 'Variegatum' is variegated. Height up to 10'.

Physalis franchetii (Chinese lantern). 'Gigantea' 3', September fruits. Hang to dry.

Phytolacca (poke-weed). *P. americana* has blackberry-type fruits (not edible) in September.

Polygonatum x. hybridum (Solomon's seal) 2'-4', June. Graceful arched stems, leaves glycerine.

Polystichum setiferum 'Divisilobum' attractive fern, good in pots.

Primula P. auricula are good for period arrangements and for pressing as are the many coloured *P. vulgaris* Pacific strain (Polyanthus). These have good stems for cutting as do *P. denticulata*, the drumstick primrose. All are low-growing and flower in Spring.

Pyrethrum daisylike long lasting when cut. 2', May/June.

Scabiosa (scabious) *S. causcasica* 18"-24", June/September. 'Penhill Blue' lavendar-blue flowers, 'Bressingham White', 'Moonstone' light blue. *S. ochroleuca*, yellow. Silica gel flowers.

Sedum (stonecrop) 1'-3' long-flowering as the flowers can be used in the early stage when green, also good foliage for cutting. *S. maximum* 'Atropurpureum' has purple leaves and stems. *S. spectabile* green leaves, pink flowers.

Sempervivum (houseleek) *S. tectorum* 'Commander Hay' has purple-red, green-tipped rosettes of leaves. Low-growing clumps, the rosettes make good centres for foliage arrangements.

Senecio maritima 'Diamond' has almost white leaves which are lovely in silver containers. Treat as an annual or take inside in colder districts. Leaves press.

Tellima grandiflora 18", small flowers. April/June but the small round leaves are excellent ground cover and useful to hide mechanics, evergreen and streaked with brown in winter. Leaves press.

Tiarella cordifolia (foam flower) 12", May/June but leaves are the most useful, maple-like, pale-green.

Trollius (globe flower) buttercup-like flowers in oranges and yellow. 2½', May/June. *T.x. hybridus* 'Lemon Queen' is pale yellow.

103

Verbascum 'Mont Blanc' (white), 'Hartleyi' (biscuit), 'Gainsborough' (yellow).

Vinca major (greater periwinkle) 6", good ground cover and useful 'trails' for arrangements. 'Variegata' is the prettiest.

Viola x. wittrockiana (pansy). Many colours, good for pressing. 'Swiss Giants' has numerous colours.

5 Shrubs

A shrub is a plant with stems which are mainly wood. It normally has many stems rather than a single trunk (as a tree) but it is not always a simple matter to say when a plant is a large shrub or a small tree.

The word 'shrub' is not a beautiful one to say and can conjure up a picture of rather untidy, poor growth which is a pity because shrubs include many very lovely plants which are the backbone of gardens. Some have wonderful colours in the

A shrub border with spaces left for annuals and dahlias. The large oval leaves are Bergenia purpurascens, *an evergreen perennial*

Autumn, some have delicate flowers, others exciting berries or fruits, there are those with fascinating bare winter branches and others which are evergreen and grace the garden the whole year round.

Once a few shrubs have been planted in a garden then it seems 'furnished' and to this basic framework can be added roses, hardy perennials, bulbs and annuals. It is also possible to have an interesting and beautiful garden which contains nothing but shrubs. Nowadays there are so many varieties that the modern shrub garden is a far cry from the gloomy Victorian shrubbery.

The disadvantage of shrubs is that they are expensive to buy and slow to grow to full size which means that they cannot be hacked with abandon for flower arrangement. However with careful cutting and limiting the use of the shrub plant material in flower arrangements to winter only, they will grow on, despite the flower arranger. The great advantage is that shrubs are very labour saving, requiring little or no work after planting and they provide plant material for arrangements when nothing else is available in the garden.

Shrub Growing

Choosing Shrubs

This needs care if money is not to be wasted. Shrubs need to be selected for their decorative value in the garden as well as their usefulness as plant material for flower arrangement. You cannot afford mistakes because of the initial high cost and because they take a long time to grow. By the time you have decided the shrub is unattractive and not much use, valuable growing time has been lost and shrubs really do take a long time to become established in the garden.

Examples of shrubs can be seen in established gardens but remember when you examine their size that those growing around stately homes may have been there for thirty years or more and this can be misleading. Many shrubs are now sold in containers at nurseries and garden centres and this is a great help as you can see what you are buying before carrying it away. Nurserymen sometimes plant a shrub border so that you can see how the mature plant will appear after a few years. There are several things to consider before buying:

1 *The type of soil in the garden*
It is sensible to find out the type of soil in your garden if you intend to plant many shrubs. Some, such as azaleas and rhododendrons, do not thrive in lime. It is easier to work *with* your soil and choose shrubs which will thrive in it, rather than to choose the shrub and then have to work hard to change the soil for it. You need to know whether the soil is acid, limey or neutral and this can be discovered easily with a small soil testing kit available at low cost from garden centres. Instructions are clearly given with the kit and you can quickly find out the degree of acidity, which is measured on what is known as the pH scale. Anything below pH 7 is acid (non-limey) and anything above is alkaline (limey). Ask the nurseryman before buying a shrub if it will thrive in your type of soil.

2 *The climate in the garden*
Until you can find out about the climate in your garden it is sensible to buy only really hardy plants. You may find it is windy, holds the frost for a long time or is very exposed.

3 *Evergreens*
It is sensible to lean towards buying evergreens rather than

Mahonia bealei, *an evergreen shrub*

deciduous shrubs if you are limited for space or money. They will look attractive in the garden all year and make it seem less bare in winter. Also evergreens provide leaves for using in flower arrangements when there is nothing else in the garden to pick.

4 *Catalogues*

'Catalogue-buying' if you are not already familiar with a shrub, or choosing from a short cut spray from a bush, is a mistake as it is important to see the shape and the size before buying. Having bought a shrub you will be stuck with it for a long time so you should be sure you like it as you will often see it from the windows of your home.

5 *Variety*

If space is freely available, plant a variety of shrubs to give something to pick all the year round.

Planting Shrubs

WHEN TO PLANT

Plant shrubs which lose their leaves in winter (deciduous) in the Autumn or Winter when the leaves are off the plant.

Plant evergreens in the Autumn or Spring. They are a little more difficult to transplant as the leaves continue to transpire all year and it is easy for the shrub to become parched. Evergreens transplant better from containers.

Plant container-grown shrubs at any time, providing the soil is not frozen, but make sure the soil around the roots is not disturbed and that it is watered especially well in dry weather.

THE SITE

Shrubs with a very good or graceful shape make attractive features in a garden and can be planted as isolated specimens, but consider the position in relation to the house before choosing a site.

A shrub border is successful using shrubs of varying sizes, shapes and colours with ground cover plants below. In this case the contours should be considered so that high shrubs go to the back and low-growing or spreading ones at the front. This gives a feeling of 'up-and-down'. Avoid planting two similar sized and shaped shrubs close together. You may want to spread the evergreens evenly around the border and to have splashes of yellow-

Cutting away the container from a shrub

The roots should not be disturbed when planting

green shrubs at intervals amongst the dark greens or grey-greens.

Many people now plant shrubs, roses and hardy perennials in one border with annuals for filling up gaps, but care must be taken to see that plants which need full sun do get it and are not shaded by the shrubs.

PREPARATION OF THE SOIL

It is important to do this well in the case of shrubs because it is the first and also the last dig over as it is unlikely that you will move shrubs.

Using a spade dig a hole big enough to take the roots without squashing them up. Put in several handfuls of peat and two large handfuls of bonemeal mixed with a handful of hoof and horn meal. The base of the hole should be higher in the centre than at the sides to prevent bending up the roots.

PLANTING

Spread the roots out naturally in the hole and place the shrub so that the old soil mark on the stem lies just below the surface of the soil. Face the shrub so that its best side faces the way that

a temporary screen can prove a great help to newly planted evergreens

it will be seen most often. Replace some of the soil and tread this in before replacing any more. Continue replacing and firming in with the feet. If the weather is dry make a 'saucer' around the plant and pour on a can of water. This makes the water stay around the shrub and not run off. Then add a mulch of peat to hold in the moisture during the summer.

DISTANCE APART

It is important to space shrubs carefully when planting otherwise some will have to be removed when fully grown. The normal height when grown is given in nursery catalogues or gardening books and a good guide is to allow at least $\frac{2}{3}$ of their normal height when fully grown between plants.

Feeding

Feed shrubs in Spring with a good handful of a general fertilizer spread around the roots and add garden compost if available.

Pruning

There are many shrubs which *never* need pruning. If in doubt *do not prune* as shrubs can grow happily on without pruning, unlike roses. The only disadvantage may be smaller flowers on a poor shape. Cutting a few stems for flower arrangements may be all that is necessary. If not then it is usually sufficient to cut back projecting branches and thin out overcrowded growth. Ask the nurseryman about pruning at the time of buying a shrub. Generally-speaking evergreen shrubs need less pruning than deciduous ones.

WHEN TO PRUNE – FLOWERING SHRUBS

The basic principle is that you prune after a flowering shrub has flowered but if it is a late flowerer then it is unwise to prune it just before the onset of cold weather and so you wait until Spring, otherwise new young growth which has been encouraged to grow will get literally 'nipped in the bud'.

Early flowering. Shorten all the stems that have just carried flowers. If possible cut immediately above a young non-flowering stem or a bud which will grow into a new stem. Prune soon after flowering, e.g. Winter jasmine.

111

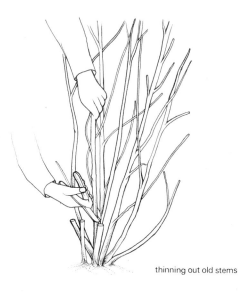

thinning out old stems

Late-flowering. Late means after mid-summer. Prune in March or April removing a few of the older branches or shorten all the branches so that strong new growth appears e.g. Buddleia. Generally shape the bush also. A few shrubs need cutting down to within a few inches of ground level but even this is not essential, e.g. Dogwood when grown for its red bark in winter.

Evergreens. Prune only if unshapely or overgrown in late Spring or early summer, or if in flower, then after flowering. Do a minimum of pruning. Cutting for arrangements is usually adequate.

Arranging Shrub Plant Material

In the Winter evergreen shrubs come into their own as material for flower arrangements as there is a limit to the number of arrangements one wants to make with flowers alone, driftwood or preserved (brown) leaves. A little yellow-green laurel or elaeagnus can work wonders for a few bought flowers, and holly and ivy are lovely for a traditional Christmas design. The flowering shrubs, such as witchhazel and camellia give a few delightful flowers in early Spring to cheer up the gloomy months. Long arching sprays of the summer flowering shrubs, such as

112

lilac, are lovely for large pedestal arrangements. When space is limited then I should choose the evergreens as they can be picked when there are few garden flowers available and combined with florist's flowers. During the summer give these shrubs a rest from cutting as there are other plants to pick and evergreen foliage can look heavy with summer flowers. Many evergreens take glycerine very well and this can be done during the summer.

Cutting

Allow your new shrubs to grow without cutting for a year or two until they are reasonably well established. When they can be cut without looking denuded, then it is important that shrubs are cut with care to encourage new growth.

1 Cut off a branch where there is another one growing close to it. This will give the remaining branch space and light to thrive.
2 Cut just above a new shoot and not below leaves because any portion of stem remaining will die. Cutting near a new shoot encourages it to grow well.
3 Think 'flower arrangement' as you cut and choose the shape and length carefully to avoid any wastage. Cut *less* than you think will be needed.

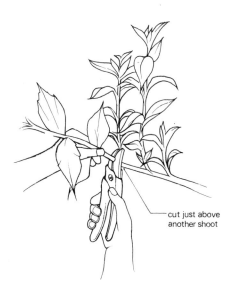

cut just above
another shoot

Cut and then if possible put the stems immediately into a bucket of warm water taken into the garden. If not and the stem has been left out of water for longer than about ten minutes, then recut the stem to remove any callus that has formed. A callus is a layer of corky tissue which forms naturally over any wound (or cut) made in a plant and it can prevent water from entering the stem.

Conditioning

Many shrubs have hard woody stems which protect them through the winter and prevent them from losing moisture. It follows that they do not allow water to go in easily from the *outside* either. For this reason it is necessary to peel back, or remove, some of the outside bark from a few inches of the stem end. This can be done with a knife and it exposes the inner tissue to the water in a container. In addition cut up the stem vertically to expose further tissue to water and if the stem is thick make several cuts. Some people hammer the ends with the same aim in mind but this makes a messy stem-end which can be difficult to impale on a pinholder. Deep water is not necessary for conditioning the stems of shrubs as long as the exposed part of the stem is standing in warm water.

If the shrub has leaves then they do need submerging to become really crisp and full of water. Push the whole stem under tepid water in a sink, or a bath, according to the size of the branch.

The flowers of some shrubs, such as lilac, soon wilt if they are cut for flower arrangement because there are often many leaves and these transpire rapidly. Removing all or most of the leaves means that the available moisture goes to the flowers and they last longer.

WILTED PLANT MATERIAL

Cut off a few inches from the stem end and put it into very hot water. Woody stems will take boiling water and this moves up the stem more rapidly than cold. About two to three inches of stem should stand in the hot water. Protect the flower heads with a cloth or paper and then leave the stems in the water until it cools. If there are many leaves then totally submerge the cutting in a bath of *tepid* water.

Mechanics

The woody or hard stems of shrubs make them especially suitable for pinholders as they are easily impaled. Sometimes the stem end may be too hard or thick to push on the pins but a few short cuts in the end should make this possible. Shrub stems also go into plastic foam well but if the stem is thick sharpen the end to a point for easy penetration.

Preservation

The foliage of many shrubs is excellent for preserving with glycerine and is often almost indestructible, lasting for many years. Hydrangea flowers dry easily as well as taking glycerine and a few flat leaves such as maple press well.

Design

The greatest value offered by shrubs is the evergreen foliage which can provide a background or framework for a few flowers in winter. Small clusters or single leaves are also excellent for hiding mechanics.

Bare branches of shrubs are invaluable for giving height to a design which uses a few Spring flowers and they are a basis for many 'line' designs in the Winter. Two or three branches with an interesting shape such as those of the contorted hazel are fascinating to have in the house combined with three or four irises or daffodils. Christmas arrangements can be made with branches sprayed with gold, copper or silver and abstract designs with straight-growing twigs such as those of dogwood.

A few flowers of the camellia give lovely emphasis to the centre of an arrangement and smaller flowers on long branches such as philadelphus give long flowing lines for large arrangements in summer. Hydrangea flowers are excellent for drawing several colours together in a design as they often show such lovely combinations of colours and are delightful for the house. The brilliant blue provide a rare chance for using green-blue which is a very scarce colour in flowers.

The following shrubs are easy to grow, hardy and useful for flower arrangement. There are of course very many others but

An economical pedestal arrangement of shrub foliage including Philadelphus
(Mock orange), Fatsia japonica *for hiding the mechanics,* Escallonia, *with a few
flowers. Arranged by Dorothy Haworth*

this is a good collection with which to start. Height at full
growth is approximate and may take a long time.

E: evergreen   D: deciduous
Acer pseudo platanus 'Brilliantissimum' (a form of maple) D. This
   is really a tree but this form is small and has lovely apricot

116

coloured leaves in Spring which hold up very well in the house. Later they turn green with white veining. Slow-grower but worth it. No pruning except by the flower arranger. Good for pressing.

Acer negundo 'Variegatum' (a form of maple) D. tree. Has green and white leaves which are useful and condition easily. No pruning. Good for pressing.

Acer platanoides (Norway maple) D. tree. Brilliant green flowers in April before the leaves.

Aucuba japonica (spotted laurel) E. 6'–12'. Very easily grown and also good in pots. 'Variegata' is a common one. 'Longifolia' has slender leaves. The leaves can be heavy looking if used on long branches but small cuttings are invaluable for hiding mechanics. The leaves glycerine dark brown and are better wired singly. No pruning necessary.

Berberis thunbergii (barberry) 4' *B. t. atropurpurea* has arching stems of maroon coloured small leaves which are useful to use with pink and red flowers. Cut older branches for lasting. No pruning except to remove old stems occasionally.

Buddleia davidii (butterfly bush) D. 9'. Fragrant flowers, slightly arching branches. 'Golden Glow' is cream-apricot, 'White Bouquet' is white and there are several violet and deep red varieties. In April cut back the previous year's growth almost to where it started to encourage large flowers.

Buddleia globosa (orange ball tree) D. 18'. Enjoyed by children as it has small, orange flowers in compact balls in June. Thin or shorten lightly after flowering.

Buxus (box) E. Small bush *B. sempervivens* 'Latifolia Maculata' has small broad leaves and is variegated yellow. The woody branches are excellent for pushing into plastic foam for 'topiary' trees and cone shaped designs. Box lasts several weeks and covers mechanics well. No pruning.

Camellia japonica E. 6'–12'. Plant in a sheltered place to avoid damage to the flowers, hardy, but wind and exposed conditions are not advisable. The early morning sun should be avoided when siting. There are many lovely varieties of early Spring flowers. Red flowered varieties stand cold better. The foliage is glossy green and long lasting in water and is very tough when glycerined. The flowers should be cut when almost fully open as buds often fail to open and should be sprayed with a fine mist of water often as the stems are very woody and

117

absorb little water. Soil should be lime-free. No pruning but remove dead flowers.

Calluna vulgaris (heather) E. Low growing, 'H. E. Beale' bright pink, large flowers which dry well by hanging. Clip in the Spring.

Cornus (dogwood) D. 10'. *C. alba* 'Sibirica', red stems and *C. stolonifera* 'Flaviramea' yellow stems – cut down hard in April to produce new coloured stems, useful for modern designs. *C. alba* 'Elegantissima', variegated. Hard prune every other year in March.

Cornus mas (Cornelian cherry) D. 15'. Very small yellow flowers on bare stems in early Spring. No pruning.

Corylus avellana 'Contorta' (Harry Lauder's walking stick) D. 12'-15'. The twisted hazel which provides excellent curved branches for winter use. Remove straight growing shoots.

Cotinus coggygria 'Folis Purpureis' (form of Smoke Bush) D. 10'. Dark plum coloured foliage. Pick older leaves for lasting well in water. Lovely if planted so that the evening sun in Autumn shows through the flame coloured leaves. No regular pruning.

Cotoneaster 'Cornubia' semi-E. 10'-15', clusters of scarlet berries in the Autumn. *C. franchetii* berries along its stem. Useful for Autumn and Winter arrangements and not usually eaten by the birds. No regular pruning. *C.* 'Rothschildianus' has clusters of yellow berries.

Cytisus (broom) D. 6'-8'. *C. albus* has useful long arching sprays for flower arrangement. It will seed itself easily. About $\frac{2}{3}$ of the stems can be cut back as far as hard wood, after flowering, to improve the shape. *C. x praecox* is an early flowering variety. Lengths of stem can be tied in circles, soaked, dried still tied up and then untied for swirls which stay curved permanently.

Elaeagnus E. 8'-12'. *E. pungens* 'Maculata' has leaves splashed with gold. 'Variegata' has narrow yellow margins and is more vigorous. Both should have any plain leafed sprays cut away. This is delightful in the winter garden and the leaves are very colourful in winter arrangements. *E. macrophylla* has green leaves with undersides of silver on arching branches. No regular pruning. Glycerines.

Euonymus fortunei 'Variegata' E. green and white climber 10'. Gives short stems of variegated foliage for Spring arrangements. Pink-tinged in Winter. No pruning.

Eucalyptus gunnii E. Needs full sun. Leaves grey-purple and last

118

well in water, also taking glycerine well. For good foliage and to avoid very tall growth which can snap in a wind, cut annual growths off in early Spring after frosts, as near as possible to the base. This makes a 'stooled' plant – (many shoots emerging from the base rather than one trunk). Good leaves for pressing.

Escallonia E. 6'–8'. *E.* 'Langleyensis' has carmine flowers in July and 'Apple Blossom' is pale pink. Good branches of small leaves all year. Glycerines. Trim lightly after flowering.

Fatsia japonica E. 8'–15'. Invaluable as a decorative garden shrub and also for flower arrangement. The bold leaves are excellent for large pedestal arrangements especially for covering mechanics. They also suit modern designs. The leaves last well in water and glycerine easily but should be submerged in the mixture or mopped well with it. Likes a sheltered, windless position and grows well in city gardens. No pruning.

x. Fatshedera E. 4'–8'. *F. lizei* 'Variegata' has leaves smaller than *Fatsia* but similar. Good in pots. It is a cross between fatsia and ivy. Cuttings grow easily and the leaves last well in water and take glycerine. No pruning, peg down if used for ground cover when 18″ long.

Garrya elliptica E. 6'–8'. Grey-green catkins November to February. The male plants have longer catkins. Needs protection in the North, such as against a wall. No pruning.

Hamamelis (witch hazel) D. 6'–8'. *H. mollis* has small strange yellow flowers in January. Slow grower but worth waiting. It should be planted near the house to enjoy the flowers. No pruning except for cutting for arrangements.

Hedera (ivy) E. climber. *H. canariensis* 'Variegata' green and grey leaves. Cuttings root quickly in water. It may be cut down by a severe Winter but grows again normally. *H. colchica* 'Dentata Aurea' is green leaved with a yellow margin. The big leaves are useful for covering mechanics and the sprays for trails in an arrangement. Long lasting in water. Glycerines. Presses.

Hydrangea D. 4'–6'. Invaluable for both garden display and flower arrangement. When chalk or lime is present they tend to be pink or red rather than blue. Flowers in July–September. The flowers can be picked when beginning to go papery in October and placed in ½″ of water to gradually dry off. They may also be glycerined (when mature but not papery) if cut on a length of woody stem. Mature flowers last far better in water than young ones. If a flower wilts submerge the head in slightly

119

warm water for an hour. See your local nursery for colours and hardiness. The leaves turn good colours in Autumn and are long lasting in water and useful for covering mechanics. Cut back each Spring.

Ilex (holly) E. 12'–20'. *I. aquifolium* 'Golden King' with gold margined leaves and 'Silver Queen' with silver edged leaves. These are both useful at Christmas. *I. aquifolium* 'Bacciflava' has yellow berries which are unusual. No pruning. Leaves like spraying indoors.

Jasminum nudiflorum (winter jasmine) D. 10'. Gives very early small yellow flowers which can be freely cut. It needs support but will grow on a North wall. Cut back flowering growths to within 2" or 3" of the base.

Laurus nobilis 'Aurea' E. small tree, light green foliage.

Ligustrum ovalifolium 'Aureo-marginatum' (golden privet) semi-E. Useful yellow-green winter foliage. No pruning unless untidy. *L. lucidum*, 'Excelsum Superbum' is very beautiful with curved branches and variegated leaves.

Liriodendron (tulip tree) D. tree, 18'. Useful yellow leaves in Autumn which will take glycerine well in summer. No pruning. *Liriodendron tulipifera* 'Aureomarginatum' has variegated foliage.

Lonicera japonica (Japanese honeysuckle) E. Climber, useful curved sprays which last well in water. Thin only.

Magnolia x. soulangeana D. 10'–15'. Spectacular tree with large white flowers, rose-purple at the base in April. Short lived flowers but dramatic in the house. No pruning.

Mahonia 'Charity' E. 8'. Handsome leaves and an attractive shrub in the garden. The foliage is invaluable all year and glycerines very well. This variety is more graceful for flower arrangement than some of the others. No pruning.

Philadelphus (mock orange) D. 'Belle Etoile' is a neat variety which has single flowers with a little purple at the centre. Remove all or most of the leaves before arranging in the house. Better flowers result from cutting back some of the flowered shoots to strong new growth. June/July flowering.

Prunus (ornamental cherry) P. 'Shimidsu Sakura' is dainty but there are so many from which to choose that it is better to see these in bloom before buying. They are not long lasting in water but lovely when picked in bud. They can be forced to open early by bringing the sprays indoors two or three weeks before normal flowering time. No pruning.

Pyracantha atalantioides (firethorn) E. 8'. Red berries in Autumn and good evergreen coverage for a North wall. 'Aurea' has yellow berries. Long sprays can be cut if you beat the birds to it. Prune by cutting long sprays and neatening the bush for flower arrangements.

Rhododendron E. acid soil. Many colours – choose smallest flowers for cutting purposes. No pruning but remove faded flowers. 'Lady Roseberry' is dainty. Remove dead flowers.

Ruta graveolens (Rue) E. Blue-green foliage which lasts well in water. Cut back in Autumn if not already cut for flower arrangements. 'Variegata' has cream and green foliage.

Salix (willow) D. tree. *S. matsudana* 'Tortuosa' has useful twisted branches for arrangements. 'Setsuka' has fasciated (flattened) Spring branches which are effective for modern designs.

Skimmia japonica E. 2'–3'. Be sure to buy a male and a female bush for the red berries in the Autumn. Dislikes lime. No pruning. Good light green leaves for covering mechanics. *S. japonica* 'Rubella' (male) *S.* 'Foremanii' (female). *S. reevesiana* is self fertile.

Sorbus (mountain ash) D. tree. *S. cashmiriana* 10'–15'. White fruit $\frac{1}{2}''$ wide lasting after the foliage has gone. *S. hupehensis* white berries with pink tinge but smaller than *S. cashmiriana*. Lovely for Autumn and Winter arrangement. No pruning. *S. aria* (common white beam) D. tree. Beautiful young silver leaves, excellent with Spring flowers. Glycerines well. Prune to control shape.

Spiraea thunbergii D. 5'. Arching branches of small white flowers in March and April. *S. x. bumalda* 'Anthony Waterer' 3', has variegated cream, green and pink foliage which should be cut down to ground level in March.

Symphoricarpos rivularis 'Constance Spry' (form of snowberry) white berries last for weeks in water. Cut out a few old stems to ground level in Spring.

Syringa (lilac) *S. persica* D. 6'–7'. 'Primrose', 'Alba' is white, small flowered panicles, *S. velutina*, dainty violet. The Canadian Hyrids are daintier than the common lilac for flower arrangement. *S. x. josiflexa* has rose-pink flowers in May and June. The leaves should be removed after cutting them for the house for a longer flower life. Cut out old wood sometimes.

Thuja occidentalis 'Rheingold' E. 6'. Slow growing but lovely bronze-yellow with tough feathery foliage which sparks up winter arrangements with its texture and colour. No pruning.

Viburnum x. bodnantense E. 9'. 'Dawn' clustered white rose-tinted flowers in March. *V. opulus* (guelder rose) D. 15', big red berries in Autumn on 'Notcutts Variety'. *V. tinus* (laurustinus) has white and pink flowers in the Winter and useful evergreen foilage. *V. plicatum* has large white (green at first) snowballs for flowers. No pruning.

Weigela florida 'Variegata' D. 6'-8'. Pale pink flowers in May and early June and leaves edged with cream. Long branches can be cut. Remove flower wood after flowering.

Choisya is a shrub with lovely rosettes of foilage but it is not hardy in the North. Clematis make wonderful climbing garden plants but the lives of the flowers are very short when cut. *Ceanothus* is an unusual blue flowered shrub but it needs protection in the North. Azaleas are lovely garden shrubs but not long lasting flowers in the house. There are many excellent shrubs which have not been mentioned and these can be seen in local nurseries.

6 Dahlias

The dahlia is a happy, undemanding flower with a range of warm colourings and an association with a time of plenty and Harvest Festivals. It originated in Mexico, being first grown by the Aztecs in the 14th century, and often has the exotic brilliance of that fascinating country. It came to Europe in 1789 and is named after Andreas Gustav Dahl, Swedish botanist.

Dahlias flower from early August until the frost blackens their leaves giving a final burst of colour before the winter sets in and

The miniature decorative dahlia 'Newby' which is a good size for flower arrangement

glowing in the garden in the late Autumn sun and the evening mists.

Dahlias grow rather like Jack's beanstalk of pantomime fame. One day there is the brown earth and in no time at all there is a veritable forest of flowers and leaves to pick and enjoy. This rapid growth is a most useful characteristic as it means dahlias can be planted to fill in spaces quickly in the Summer garden. They also flower freely and 'cut-and-come-again' is an apt description for the flower arranger need have no fear, when picking dahlias, that the garden will be denuded of colour.

Plants and tubers are inexpensive and will grow easily in a variety of places and soils. A minimum of effort is needed for a good display and they are also easily propagated. For these reasons dahlias are extremely popular for massing in beds, especially in parks and on estates. In a home garden I think they look better mixed with other plants in shrub borders or perennial beds where they give colour and substance during the late Summer and Autumn.

The dahlia is a tender plant which does not normally survive

A dahlia tuber

the winter if left out in the garden. It is a half-hardy tuberous perennial with fleshy swollen roots which form a lump at the base of the stem. These are called tubers and they act as storage organs allowing the plant to rest without any harm, even though it has no water or food. In the winter the dahlia becomes dormant and can be lifted, kept in a sheltered place and brought into life again the following summer.

Growing Dahlias

Buying Dahlias

Dahlias are bought as rooted cuttings or tubers. They should be ordered from reputable nurserymen after seeing them in flower if possible, during the previous summer. Flower shows, nurseries and parks are good places to visit. There are many varieties from which to choose and the colour of the flower and the size of both the flower and the plant need consideration before buying. Catalogues give details and pictures and, as dahlias photograph well, catalogue-buying is more reliable than it is for most other plants.

Most of the large and giant varieties are unsuitable for the average garden and their flowers are too big for using in arrangements in the home. Medium, small and miniature varieties are the better choice.

VARIETIES

All dahlia flowers are round but they differ in the formation of their petals and there are many colours, mostly brilliant. The names of the various groups can be hard to remember but the following brief descriptions should be helpful.

CACTUS

The petals are narrow and rolled or tubular for at least half their length and the flower has a spikey appearance overall. Semi-cactus have broader petals which are semi-rolled for less than half their length.

DECORATIVE

The many petals are broad, flat and usually blunt at the tips. This is a most useful group for cut flowers. Some, with very

125

broad petals, are called 'Water-lily' and are especially loved by flower arrangers.

SINGLED-FLOWERED

There is just one row of petals around a central disc. They may be grown from seed and are cheap. They are useful for dark parts of the garden and under trees but are poor cut flowers as they fade quickly indoors.

ANEMONE-FLOWERED

This is a small group similar to single-flowered dahlias but having a ring of short florets around the central disc, often of a contrasting colour. They are sometimes known as 'pincushion Dahlias' and last quite well in water.

COLLERETTE

These are single dahlias with a central disc and a ring of smaller petals attached to the outer petals and about half their length. This ring gives them the name 'Collerette' and it is often a different colour, which can make them a rather exciting flower. They are quite good for cutting.

PAEONY-FLOWERED

This might be called a 'double' single as it has two or more rows of petals around the central disc. Lasts fairly well in water.

BALL

These are ball-shaped flowers sometimes flattened on the top. The petals are blunt or rounded at the tips. The sides of the florets curve inwards for more than half their length. They make very good cut flowers.

POMPON

These are similar flowers to 'Ball' but more globular and much smaller. The florets curve inwards along their whole length. This is a delightful small dahlia which is invaluable for the flower arranger.

A medium semi-cactus dahlia

'Twiggy', a small decorative dahlia

'Comet', an anenome-flowered dahlia

A miniature ball dahlia

Planting

THE SITE

Dahlias grow better in a sunny position but a partially shaded position is quite satisfactory. They need sunshine at some period of the day but the aspect is immaterial. They will not grow well under large trees with roots that take up all the surrounding moisture.

PREPARATION OF THE SOIL

The usual 'dig-over', adding compost if possible is desirable plus a weathering for a week or two, before planting. However dahlias can go straight into an existing bed. Clear any weeds beforehand.

WHEN TO PLANT

Unspouted tubers – early May.
Rooted cuttings and sprouted tubers – early June.

HOW TO PLANT – TUBERS

Dig a hole large enough for the tuber and place a cane at the back of the hole, which should not be so deep that the main stem in the centre of the dahlia is covered. This should stand up out of the ground, when the soil is replaced. Press the soil firmly over the tuber, making a saucer or shallow bowl around the protruding stem as this will direct water towards it. Scatter a handful of bonemeal over the buried tuber. This can be watered in, if the weather is dry, but do not use a tool to work it in as this can damage the tuber. In a few weeks green shoots will appear through the ground from the base of the stem. (They do not arise from the tuber.) When about 6″ high tie them loosely to the cane.

ROOTED CUTTINGS

These are usually sold in containers. If these are of plastic they must be removed but if they are made of paper or fibre they can be left to support the soil around the roots. It is better to remove the bottom of the container and slit up the sides to avoid restricting growth. Dig a hole big enough to take the roots, place a cane in the back of the hole, throw a handful of bonemeal into the hole and place the plant in front of the cane. The soil around the

Flowers for a special occasion. The stems were inserted into soaked plastic foam impaled on a long, oval-headed nail on top of a 14″ length of broomstick. Plaster of Paris holds the stick in a plastic pot.

Annual flowers, grasses and seedheads in the manner of a Flemish flower painting of the 17th and 18th centuries, with grapes and shells as accessories.

A planted tuber

roots should be immediately below the level of the soil in the bed. Firm the plant down by pressing with the feet and scoop a saucer around the plant so that when watering on dry summer days, the water stays around the plant and does not trickle off into the desert of dry soil in the flower bed. Tie the plant *loosely* to the cane for support using garden string.

Care of Dahlias

STOPPING

It seems rather drastic to pinch off the growing tip (that is the top) of a plant but it is essential if a good bushy plant with many flowers is required. This pinching off induces side shoots to grow. If the growing tip is missing when the plant is bought, then stopping may have been already done at the nursery. It is usual to do this when the plant has formed four good pairs of leaves. Be brave and take off the top just above a good pair of leaves and before long some side shoots will appear.

Supporting a dahlia plant

SUPPORTING

The first cane placed in position when planting is sufficient support at first. It is essential to push this in position *before* planting the tuber or plant so that there is no damage to the roots. When the dahlia is about 18″ in height it will need further support as the soft stems of dahlias are easily broken by the wind. Push two more canes, making three in all, into the ground about 6″–9″ away from the plant in a triangle. Cut a good length of garden string and loop it around a stem approximately 18″ above the ground. Cross over the ends and then tie them around a cane. As the plants grow one or two further ties may be necessary. This support should withstand any howling gales.

THINNING

Some stems will grow more strongly than others. Very weak stems should be removed at the base of the plant leaving about three strong stems into which goes the energy of the plant.

DISBUDDING

If especially good flowers are required the number of buds can be reduced but this is not necessary if you would rather have more flowers for cutting. At the end of each branch three buds

130

appear and the two outer ones can be removed leaving one strong one.

WATERING

Dahlias grow rapidly from the middle of July and require a lot of water. Give them an occasional good soak if the weather is dry.

DEADHEADING

Remove dead flowers by cutting the stem off above the joint. This encourages new shoots and flowers to grow.

FEEDING

This is not necessary if compost was added to the ground previously and bonemeal at planting time, but an occasional application of liquid fertiliser will keep the plants going and maintain flower size to the end of the season.

LIFTING AND STORING

When frost has blackened the leaves and stopped further growth, cut the stems down to about 6″ above the ground. Push a garden

A tuber turned upside down to drain after lifting

fork into the soil – it may be necessary to do this in more than one place to loosen the tuber – and then holding the stems gently ease the tuber from the ground and shake off the soil. Place the tuber upside down under cover for a week to drain off any moisture in the hollow stems. Place the lifted tubers in shallow boxes containing dry peat, or wrap them in newspaper, and store then in a frost-proof place with a temperature around 5°C (41°F). No cover is needed.

PROPAGATING DAHLIAS

This is easy and fun too, giving many new plants at no expense.

DIVISION OF TUBERS

In mid-April, place the tuber in a shallow box containing moist peat and sand in equal quantities. Leave the crown clear. Keep the soil moist and after two or three weeks green shoots will appear. Divide the tuber with a sharp knife leaving a portion of tuber and one shoot or growth bud on each piece cut away. Plant out with the base of the shoot at least 3″ below ground in early June.

CUTTINGS

The thought of taking cuttings alarms many people but in the case of dahlias it is a simple matter and gives a great sense of achievement. Start the tuber growing at the beginning of April in a box of moist peat, as described before for tuber division. Water if the peat starts to dry out and keep in a temperature which is not below 7°C (45°F). The ideal temperature is 15–18°C (59–64°F). Shoots appear from the base of the stem and when 3″ long cut them off, discarding any large fleshy growths. Remove the lower pair of leaves from the cutting, trim the bottom of each cutting, and if possible dip the end in hormone rooting powder. Insert about four cuttings around the edge of 3″ diameter pots containing John Innes No. 1. The pots should be kept at a temperature of between 15–18°C (59–64°F) and be shaded from the sun. Water when the soil appears dry. The cuttings can be given their own little climate by shading the pot in a much larger pot one-third full of moist peat. Place a piece of glass over the top. Roots should form in ten days. Three or four weeks later pot the cuttings, which should have grown good

Shoots appearing from a tuber
Cuttings under glass

roots, singly into 3″ diameter pots and keep in a frost-proof place
until they can be planted outside in early June.

Calendar

May	Plant dormant tubers outside.
June	Plant rooted cuttings or sprouted tubers outside.
October	Lift tubers.
early April	Start tubers for cuttings.
April	Start tubers for division.

Arranging Dahlias

The great advantage of a dahlia plant for the flower arranger is
that it produces so many flowers but the disadvantage is that

they are all of an emphatic round shape with long bare stems, and they usually look better arranged with the leaves and, or, flowers of other plants. They are ideal for modern designs and those needing brilliant colours. There are many very large flowered varieties which are of little use in flower arrangement but the pompons, ball, smaller decorative and cactus groups are excellent. Their cheapness makes them excellent for decorating purposes in a large hall, a church at Harvest Festival time, or a home for special occasions.

CUTTING

Take a bucket half-full of warm water into the garden. Cut flowers which are three-quarters open to give a longer life in the house. Cutting just above a pair of leaves will encourage new stems to grow. Shake gently to remove any caterpillars, which love dahlias.

Conditioning

Dahlias have hollow stems and it can be helpful to long life to fill these with water before placing them in a decorative container. Turn the stem with the hollow end upwards, fill with water, using a watering can. (If the stem is narrow a funnel is helpful.) Plug the stem end with a piece of cotton wool and place it back in the bucket of water.

If the stem is recut when arranging the flowers, this filling and plugging should be repeated. Dahlias do last well without doing this slightly tedious job, but it is useful when the flowers have to last a long time.

WILTING DAHLIAS

Placing in warm, deep water is usually a successful method of reviving dahlias which have been out of water for a time and look limp. However towards the end of the season they do not last as well and the petals drop quickly.

Transporting

Dahlias are better carried in water otherwise they soon become limp. Care should be taken not to knock them as they do shatter easily. This can be avoided by cutting young flowers.

Mechanics

A pinholder, plastic foam or wire netting are all suitable for the stems of dahlias.

Preserving

Ball and pompon dahlias may be preserved in a silica gel with some success. The smaller firm flowers are the most suitable. Remove the stem and push a wire through the centre of the flower, turning over a hook which is pulled down into the flower. Place the flower face down in the desiccant with the new 'wire' stem sticking up.

Design

The problem with dahlias is that they are rather heavy-looking rounded flowers and can give a static appearance. They are most effective when just two or three are used in a design with other plant material where they form wonderful emphasis points or centres of interest. When an arrangement is made using nothing but dahlias only two or three should face frontwards and the others should be gradually turned away from the centre. This gives a more interesting appearance and a better sense of depth. Unfortunately big, round dahlias are often arranged in a row all facing frontwards and without any foliage. The result is an effect of garish blobs sticking straight up in a container which is most unattractive. The stems are often bare of foliage and this makes them useful for modern arrangements in which a round shape is needed without any softening leaves on the stem.

STYLES

Dahlias combine well with driftwood in line arrangements using only two or three flowers. They are also excellent for decorative abstract designs because they are of such definite shape and brilliance and can be formed into patterns with other plant material very well.

Mass designs look better when the flowers are well turned so that few face forward. Alternatively really lovely effects can be obtained with dahlias of various sizes, using pompon and ball

Dahlias need the foliage of other plants. Iris and laurel leaves give a change of shape in this design

The circular form of a dahlia flower is effective in modern designs. This arrangement includes driftwood, bulrushes and a glycerined Bergenia *leaf to echo the design on the container*

varieties on the outside of the designs and a few small or miniature decorative or cactus varieties in the centre.

COMBINING WITH OTHER PLANT MATERIAL

The foliage of dahlias is not very good either for its design qualities or for its lasting properties. For this reason dahlias are often combined with other plant material. They are movingly beautiful used with autumn leaves which are turning colour, such as those of hydrangea, azalea or the yellow autumn leaves of the tulip tree. But there are many wonderfully coloured leaves in the autumn which can be combined with dahlias to give some of the most glowing and vibrant colour schemes possible in flower arrangement. Reds, purples, oranges, yellows, browns, pinks can be put together with happy abandon.

Fruit is especially suitable for using with dahlias and flowing designs can be made giving an impression of harvests and fruitful growth. Apples, blackberries, corn, pears, gourds, plums, grapes can all be used with success. The fruit can be arranged in groups, or impaled, wired on sticks, into the mechanics.

CONTAINERS

Baskets, modern pottery, metals, are all suitable, although only dahlias in the daintier colours and smaller sizes seem to suit traditional containers of fine china.

There are many varieties, colours and sizes in dahlias and it is wise to choose those which suit your own home and colour preference. These are just a few which are useful as cut flowers.

POMPON

Andrew Lockwood, lilac
Little Conn, dark red
Moor Place, deep purple
Pom of Poms, scarlet
Rhondda, lilac, white centre
Rothesay Superb, red
Willo's night, darkest crimson
Willo's Violet, purple

BALL

Bernard Colwyn Hayes, deep pink
Esmonde, yellow

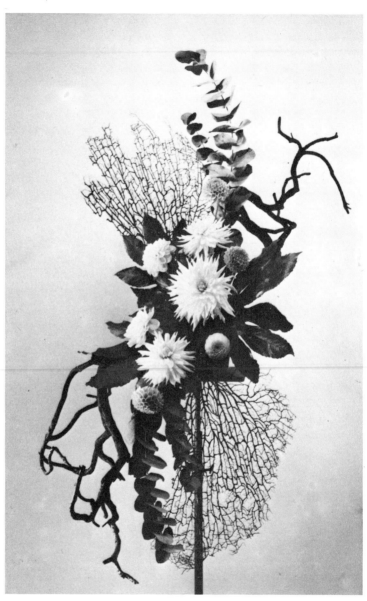

Above: *Flame coloured dahlias arranged with black wood and fan coral, and preserved* eucalyptus *and* fatsia japonica *leaves*

Opposite top: *The studio setting*

Opposite bottom: *On location for the dahlia programme*

Gloire de Lyon, white
Swiss Miss, miniature, deep pink

DECORATIVE

Angora, white, fimbriated petals, small
Chinese Lantern, orange-red, small
David Howard, orange-bronze, medium with bronze foliage
Dedham, small, lilac and white
Doris Duke, pink, miniature
Gerrie Hoek, pink, waterlily, small
Hamari Bride, white, medium
Jo's Choice, scarlet, small
Glorie van Heemstede, yellow-pink, waterlily, small
Golden Turban, yellow-orange, medium
Newby, miniature, rose-pink
Rose Newby, miniature, peach
Terpo, dark red, medium
Twiggy, shell pink, small

CACTUS

Apache, bright red, medium
Cheerio, red-tipped white, semi-cactus
Doris Day, red, small
Firestone, scarlet, semi-cactus
Klankstad Kerkrade, yellow, small
Rotterdam, red, semi-cactus

MISCELLANEOUS

Bambi, anemone-centred, yellow
Bishop of Llandaff, peony flowered, red with purple leaves
Can-Can, collerette, pink petals, yellow centre
Claire de Lune, collerette, yellow and cream
Comet, anemone-flowered, maroon
Giraffe, orchid type, orange spotted crimson, small flower
Nonsense, collerette, cream
Pink Giraffe, orchid type, pink with red spots, small flower

Group	Height of plant	Diameter of flower	Planting distance
Cactus			
medium	$3\frac{1}{2}'-4\frac{1}{2}'$	$8''-10''$	$3'$
small	$3\frac{1}{2}'-4'$	$4''-6''$	$2\frac{1}{2}'$
miniature	$3'-4'$	up to $4''$	$2\frac{1}{2}'$
Decorative			
medium	$3\frac{1}{2}'-4'$	$6''-8''$	$3'$
small	$3\frac{1}{2}'-4'$	$4''-6''$	$2\frac{1}{2}'$
miniature	$3'-4'$	up to $4''$	$2\frac{1}{2}'$
Single	$1\frac{1}{2}'-2\frac{1}{2}'$	$4''$	$1\frac{1}{2}'$
Anemone-flowered	$2'-3\frac{1}{2}'$	$4''$	$2'$
Collerette	$2\frac{1}{2}'-4'$	$4''$	$2'$
Paeony-flowered	$3'$	$4''$	$2'$
Ball	$3'-4'$	$4''-6''$	$2\frac{1}{2}'$
miniature	$3'-4'$	up to $4''$	$2\frac{1}{2}'$
Pompon	$3'-4'$	up to $2''$	$2\frac{1}{2}'$

7 Flowers from Seed

Annuals

Annuals are gay, delightful flowers, much loved by children who often start their later love of flowers and gardening with a small packet of annual seeds. An annual is a plant which grows, flowers and dies within one year. They are the cheapest flowers to grow and are useful for filling in the empty spaces in flower beds and shrub borders. This makes them invaluable for new gardens as they can provide needed colour and fill up bare beds waiting to be planted with permanent shrubs, roses and hardy perennials. They also fill in spaces between plants which are very young and to some extent prevent weeds. Apart from the utilitarian value, they are fun. New varieties can be tried without any great expense and one can proudly boast 'I grew those from seeds'. Actually they are very easy to grow and suffer little from pests and diseases because of their short lives. The flowers, which appear very quickly after sowing (about twelve weeks), endear them to children who like immediate results. There are:

Hardy annuals. The seeds may be sown out-of-doors without protection in most areas of the British Isles.
Half-hardy annuals. The seeds must be sown in a warm place and the young plants need protection until strong enough to be planted out-of-doors during the summer.

Varieties

There are very many from which to choose. Some are not suitable for flower arrangement because they wilt quickly, but there are many which provide useful cut flowers and a group that are invaluable for drying for use in winter arrangements.

Growing Annuals

Buying Seed

Many shops sell packets of seed in the Spring and the pictures on the front of the packets look so wonderful that one is tempted to buy far too many. Unfortunately the results are not always as marvellous as the pictures. It is advisable to read the words on the back before buying. This will give hints on cultivation and state whether the plants are hardy or half-hardy. As half-hardy annuals must be started in a warm place it is necessary to consider how many window-sills you can spare for the project if you do not own a green-house. Hardy annuals can go straight into the ground which is far less trouble. Read also of the size and colour of the plant so that correct positions can be allocated in the garden. Fresh seeds should be used and not old packets, for more reliable results. Well illustrated and extremely tempting catalogues are supplied by seed firms and again it is easy to overdo the order.

Seeds are usually packaged loose in the envelope, but the tiniest ones are placed in a second envelope as sometimes they can barely be seen. Seeds may also be purchased in capsules or pellets and these are placed in the ground where they dissolve, leaving the seed growing. The advantage is that the seeds can be properly spaced which saves thinning out later. There are also strips of seeds, spaced correctly. The strip is planted and dissolves leaving the seed behind.

Hardy Annuals

WHEN TO SOW

1 They may be sown out-of-doors in Spring without protection for summer flowering the same year. The word 'Spring' on the packet is vague. Mid-March is alright in warm parts of the country, April where it is colder and even early May if the Spring is cold and wet.
2 A few can be grown out-of-doors in August or September which results in small plants which grow before the winter starts, stop growing during the cold months and then grow

rapidly to flower in late Spring or early Summer. Examples are cornflowers, calendulas, *gypsophila elegans*, larkspurs, nigella.

THE SEED-BED

Most hardy annuals grow in any soil. Heavy wet soils which cake are not as satisfactory as lighter types but the soil can always be improved by working in peat. It is important that the surface of the seed bed is fine and not lumpy before it receives the seed. Dig or fork over the bed and leave it to settle for a week. Then tread it down well, wearing heavy shoes which consolidates the ground and makes it reasonably even. Scatter a handful of bonemeal to approximately one square yard of bed and rake it over in different directions to distribute the bonemeal and to get a loose crumbly surface on the soil.

SOWING LOOSE SEED

The seed can be sown in drills (lines) or scattered thinly over the bed (broadcasting). Drills are probably the easiest and the 'line' appearance is soon removed when the plants are thinned out. It is easier to identify the weeds if the seedlings are in a straight line.

SOWING IN DRILLS

Place a flat piece of wood on the prepared ground and draw a shallow line along it with a stick at right angles to the bed. For small seeds draw the drill only about $\frac{1}{4}''$ deep and for large ones about $\frac{3}{4}''$. Make the drills 6″–12″ apart according to the variety of flower. A plant which will eventually grow 6″ high (it says on the packet) should have drills 6″ apart and one growing 9″ high should have drills 9″ apart and so on. The stick with which you draw the drills can be marked with 6″, 9″, 12″ before you start sowing. Pour the seeds into the hand and then scatter gently down the drill. They can be sown from the packet but sometimes a heap drops out at once and then they are difficult to separate.

Cover the sown seeds by raking soil over them thinly. Rake *with* the drills and not across them, which scatters the seed.

THINNING OUT

This is really the only work connected with hardy annuals other than the initial sowing. Thinning out means separating plants

Treading down a seedbed
Drawing a drill
Sowing seeds

145

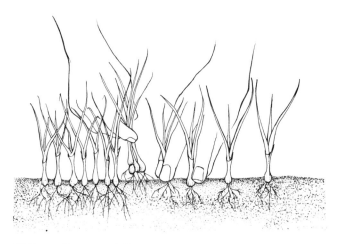

thinning seedlings sown outside

which are growing very close together when they are about 1″ high. A common mistake is to allow annuals to grow crowded together – they need space, just as people do, or they become starved and have poor flowers. The plants should be spaced about 6″ apart or a little more if they are taller growing varieties. Some annuals have tap-roots (a strong root growing vertically downwards, dandelions are an example) and these do not transplant well so they should be sown well apart, and the seed packet will give instructions about this.

SUMMER CARE

Little care is needed beyond weeding by hand or hoeing gently around the plants. Watering will be necessary in dry weather and this is better done with a fine spray as otherwise a heavy jet of water dislodges the annuals. Most annuals need to be pinched back to encourage more branches and to make them compact rather than leggy. This means cutting off the growing tips when they are 4″–5″ tall. One pinching is usually enough. Faded flowers should be removed before they produce seeds as then the life of the plant will soon be over. Removing faded flowers makes the plant produce further flowers. Birds enjoy eating young seedlings for a change of diet and some protection is needed in the early stages. Place short sticks in the ground and crisscross cotton from one to the other across the seeds. Heavy feeding of annuals is not necessary as a rich soil sometimes encourages leaves at the expense of flowers. The bonemeal scattered at planting time will probably be sufficient.

HARDY ANNUALS AS POT PLANTS

Hardy annuals may be grown indoors in pots on window-sills by those without gardens, or they can be sown in August or September for Spring-flowering in pots. See the method under half-hardy annuals.

Half-hardy Annuals

WHEN TO SOW

Half-hardy annuals need about seven weeks from sowing time to planting-out time, which is usually about the end of May for safe weather conditions. So early April sowing is time enough. They normally flower in two to three months from the date of sowing. The difference between hardy and half-hardy annuals is that the seeds of the latter will not germinate (sprout) unless they are in a warm place. A temperature of about 15°C (59°F) is desirable. It is therefore quite possible to sow them in the house if you have no greenhouse. Light is needed and a window-sill is ideal but full sun should be avoided.

SOWING THE SEED

Buy some John Innes (or similar) seed compost and some peat. Moisten the peat and place a layer on the bottom of a seed tray

Place peat in a pot

Firm down the compost

or pot. A polythene one with holes in the bottom is the most suitable as the soil in wooden ones dries out more quickly. The holes in the bottom ensure good drainage. Broken crocks or plant pots are unnecessary underneath the peat in plastic trays or pots which should be filled with John Innes seed compost to within ½″ of the top. *Firm down well* with a piece of wood or a tin lid. Water well *before* sowing the seed. Let the water settle in the compost and then scatter the seed over the surface. Large seeds can be spread over the top of the soil but tiny seeds can only be scattered, as they are too small to place in position. Cover

Sow seeds

Sieve soil over the seeds

the seeds *thinly* with fine soil. This can be sieved through an ordinary household flour sieve. It is a great mistake to cover the seeds deeply which makes it too difficult for them to struggle through the depths of soil to the surface. Very small seeds need not be covered at all.

It is necessary to cut down evaporation of moisture from the surface of the soil as this will prevent germination so the tray or pot should be covered with a piece of glass. Polythene sheeting is not always successful as it holds too much moisture and is inclined to encourage mildew and then germination does not occur. Cover the glass with brown paper or newspaper to cut down the light as germination is more likely to start in the dark, but remove the paper as soon as the seeds start to sprout. Small seedlings may then have the glass partially removed to allow

149

Cover the pot with glass and paper

ventilation, but the taller ones will need the glass entirely removed. Plastic propagators can be bought which are high enough to allow the plants to grow up and which have ventilating holes in the top. Keep the seedlings in a light place. They need soil, water, light and air in order to grow. Dry soil should be watered and this is most easily done, without damage to the tender seedlings, by means of the type of spray used for spraying a fine film of water over flowers in an arrangement and the soil should not be flooded. Alternatively the seed tray can be lowered

seed pans may be watered by standing
them in water for a few minutes

gently into a sink of water keeping the seedlings above water level. The seedlings should never be placed in hot sunshine as they will soon dry up. Check every day to see if the soil is becoming too dry.

PRICKING OUT

It is necessary to space out seedlings after they have started to grow, if they are close together. This should be done after the second pair of leaves appear. Two seed leaves grow first and when these have developed a second pair appears. This is usually the time to prick out, and it is a job for the member of the family who does not mind fiddley tasks. One seed tray may be pricked out into two or three boxes (another reason for not buying too many seeds in the first place). Separate the seedlings using a small teaspoon or stick to lift them and insert the roots into holes made with a pencil in a second tray of John Innes compost. Plant them about 2″ apart which will mean about thirty to a box. Keep the tray in a warm place for another week.

HARDENING OFF

This term gradually adjusting plants to cooler temperatures than those in which they started life. At first the seedlings should be

151

Planting seeds in peat pots

removed to a cooler but sheltered place. They may then be placed out-of-doors in warm weather but taken in at night. Gradually exposure to the outside air is increased. Any stoppage of growth or blueing or yellowing of foliage indicates that the plants have been exposed to cold air too quickly. A cold frame is useful for this stage of raising plants. By the end of May the plants should be conditioned to the open air – this may be earlier in the South – and can be planted out in the open. If this is done too soon they can be setback for some time and never reach the flowering stage.

PLANTING OUTSIDE

Fork and rake the outside bed but the soil need not be as fine and crumbly as for seeds. Plant with a small trowel or large spoon. Firm in well and water when necessary. Large seeds and small seedlings may be planted into peat pots and these may be placed straight into the open ground after hardening off. There is less disturbance for the plant in this way.

SEEDS FOR CHILDREN

Children love to grow plants from seeds and they can be given a small patch of garden as their own. It is necessary to help them select hardy annuals which are easy to grow to avoid any disappointment if the seeds do not come up. Annuals can be combined with a few plants such as pansies, and other easily grown perennials and the result will be flowers that they can cut for their own arrangements. This does not upset the senior gardeners in the family because children do love to pick flowers. A few flowers grown especially for drying and pressing can give them an occupation indoors in the winter. Many seed firms sell packets of mixed seeds which are reliable for children's gardens.

LABELLING

All seed boxes need labelling as it is so easy to forget what is in each tray and many seedlings look alike to start with.

Biennials

Biennials live for two years but only flower in the second year. They can be sown in May or June, mostly out-of-doors and then thinned out into the permanent planting position where they will flower in September.

Perennials

These are plants with a lifespan of longer than two years. They can be raised from seed but few of them flower in the first year. Most people prefer to buy established plants for quicker flowering.

Bedding Out

Annuals as small plants are offered for sale at reasonable prices by nurserymen in the Spring and early Summer. They are usually called Spring bedding plants or Summer bedding plants according to whether they flower in the Spring or Summer. If you forget or have no time or inclination to sow seeds, annuals can be bought for immediate planting out-of-doors. This should not be done until frosts are well over but it is usually advisable to order them ahead of time. It is a more expensive method of growing annuals but it is easy.

Calendar

March–April	Sow half-hardy annuals in a warm place
April–May	Sow hardy annuals out-of-doors
	Harden off half-hardy annuals
May–June	Plant out half-hardy annuals
August	Sow biennials

Arranging Annuals

Not all annuals are suitable as cut flowers for the house as they can wilt quickly. During their short lives they have little time to develop strong tissues in the stem and so their response to lack of water is a quick flop. However there are many varieties which do not wilt and they look lovely combined with perennials, with the foliage of shrubs, with driftwood or arranged alone. The foliage is seldom usable as it is somewhat limp when cut and unexciting in shape and so it is better combined with the foliage of perennials such as *Hosta* or *Alchemilla mollis*. It is a happy thought when arranging annuals to remember how little they have cost.

Cutting

Cutting flowers from annuals is good for the plant as it prevents seeds from forming and encourages a second crop of flowers. They should be cut in the bud stage to give a longer life in the house.

The stems are very soft and soon wilt so it is advisable to cut them in the early morning when the plant holds the most moisture. Collect the stems with a bucket half-full of tepid water.

Conditioning

Fill the bucket with water when the flowers reach the house so that the stems are completely submerged and leave them for about an hour to fill with water. No further conditioning is necessary unless the stem ends have been out of water for some

154

time, in which case they should be recut, preferably under water to remove any callus which has formed or an air bubble.

WILTING

Flowers which have wilted in an arrangement should be removed and the stem end should be recut under water. Stand the stem in warm water for an hour to encourage recovery, but if the plant is still floppy it is not worth going to any more trouble as the annual's lifespan is short anyway.

Mechanics

The soft stems of some varieties can prove difficult to push into plastic foam and may be better on a pinholder or in wire netting. If stems are very slender and difficult to impale on a pinholder it is helpful to insert a hollow stem onto the pinholder and slip the annual's slender stem into it for support.

Preserving

Few annuals can be preserved with glycerine but there is an excellent group for drying by the hanging method and many can be pressed for flower pictures.

Design

There are many varieties of shape, colour and texture. Short-lived annuals are better arranged quickly and simply and not 'laboured'. They can be arranged alone to emphasise their brilliant colours or they can be mixed with any other plant material.

The following plants are all useful for cutting but in addition they may dry, preserve or press well and this is stated.

HA   Hardy annual
HHA   Half-hardy annual
B   Biennial

The number refer to the eventual height of the plant.

Flowers and Seedheads for Drying

Amaranthus caudatus (love-lies-bleeding) HHA. 24". Crimson and green varieties. Long graceful tails to drop down the sides of a container, flowers dry.

Ammobium alatum (winged everlasting) HHA. 18". Silver white petals and domed yellow centre, flowers dry.

Angelica archangelica (holy ghost) B. 5'. Green flowers, seedheads dry.

Datura stramonium (thorn apple) HHA. 18". Dry the seedheads.

Delphinium solida (larkspur) HA. 36". Useful tall flower, red, pink, blue, mauve, white, flowers dry.

Dipsacus (Fuller's teasel) B. Decorative seedheads.

Helianthus annuus (sunflower) HA. Very large yellow flowers, seedhead dries.

Helichrysum (everlasting or straw flower) HHA. 12". Many colours, flowers dry.

Helipterum roseum HHA. 15". Rose and white coloured flowers, daisy shape, flowers dry.

Limonium sinuatum (statice) HHA. 18". Flowers dry.

Lunaria annua (honesty) B. 30". Silver seedheads dry, useful winter foliage.

Nicandra physaloides (shoo fly) HA. 36". Seedheads dry.

Nigella damascena (love-in-a-mist) HA. 18". Seedhead dries.

Onopordum acanthium (scotch thistle) B. 6' Grey leaves, dry flowers.

Papaver somniferum (opium poppy) HA. 30". Seedheads for drying.

Xeranthemum annuum HA. 24". Flowers dry.

Grasses for Drying

Agrostis nebulosa (cloud grass) HA. 1½'.
Briza maxima (quaking grass) HA. 18". Pendant, nodding.
Bromus macrostachys (ornamental oats) HA. 18".
Eragrostis elegans (love grass) HA. 24".
Hordeum jubatum (squirrel-tail grass) HA. 18".
Lagurus ovatus (hare's tail) HA. 18".
Panicum violaceum HA. 36".
Pennisetum longistylum HHA. 24".

156

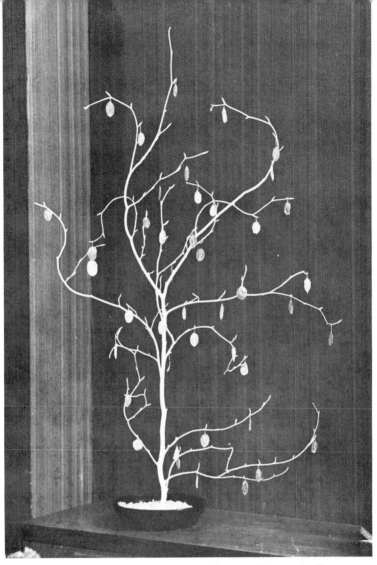

Seedheads of honesty, a biennial, glittered by glueing and dipping in glitter powder, hung with cotton on a beech branch, painted white

Setaria italica 24″. Pendant orange and tan.
Setaria glauca (yellow bristle grass) HHA. 18″.
Tricholaena rosea HHA. 24″. Wine coloured spikes.
Triticum spelta (ornamental wheat) HA. 24″.
Zea japonica variegata (ornamental corn) HHA. 4′. Foliage striped

green and white. Packets of mixed ornamental grass seeds are
also available.

Plants for Pressing

Arctotis Hybrids HHA. 18″. Several colours.
Chrysanthemum carinatum (annual chrysanthemum) HA. 18″.
The variety 'Monarch Court Jesters' has many colours, low
growing and good for pots, daisy type flower.
Coreopsis tinctoria HA. 24″. Yellow flowers.
Cosmos HHA. 36″. The variety 'Bright Lights' is orange and
scarlet, good for pots.
Humulus japonicus variegata (variegated hop) HA. Climber, green
and cream leaves for pressing.
Nicotiana affinis (tobacco plant) HHA. 30″. The varieties 'Sensa-
tion Mixed' and 'Lime Green' are useful.
Papaver nudicaule (Iceland poppy) HA. 24″. Many colours.
Phlox drummondii HHA. 15″. 'Twinkle' in mixed colours is 6″
high and good for pots, press single flowers.
Salpiglossis HHA. 2′. Many colours. Press flowers.
Tithonia (Mexican sunflower) HHA. 36″. Brilliant orange flower.

Plants for Silica Gel

Calendula (English marigold) HA. 24″. Many colours 'Whitemost'
is more green then cream, good for pots. 'Campfire', deep
orange, 'Chrysantha', yellow, 'Indian Maid', light orange,
dark centre, 'Radio', bright orange quilled petals.
Cosmos HHA. 36″.
Dianthus barbatus (sweet William) B. 12″.
Tithonia (Mexican sunflower) HHA. 36″.
Zinnia elegans HHA. 24″. 'Envy' is green but there are many
colours. 'Thumbelina' is a useful small one.

Other Useful Annuals

Antirrhinum HHP. 30″. Double 'Madame Butterfly' has many
colours; a useful tall flower.
Callistephus (China aster) HHA. 24″. A mixed seed packet gives
many varieties.

158

Centaurea cyanus (cornflower) HA. 18″. Mixed seed packet for many varieties.

Clarkia elegans HA. Mixed seed packet for many colours.

Cucurbita pepo (ornamental gourd) HHA. Climber but can be grown on the ground. Mixed seed packets give several varieties. Dry the fruit in an airing cupboard when ripe.

Digitalis (foxglove) B. 30″. Glycerine when a few flowers are left on the stem, useful tall stems.

Gaillardia HA. 24″. Red and yellow daisy flower.

Gypsophila elegans HA. 24″. Tiny white or pink flowers.

Lathyrus odoratus (sweet pea) HA. Climber, many colours.

Matthiola (annual stock) HHA. 18″. Many colours in mixed packets, good for pots.

Moluccella laevis (bells of Ireland) HHA. 18″. Glycerine or dry for honeycoloured stems.

Flowering cabbage B. 10″. Useful foliage.

Flowering kale B. 30″. Useful foliage.

Reseda odorata (mignonette) HA. 24″. 'Machet' has red ringed green flowers.

Ricinus communis 'Gibsonii' (castor oil plant) HHA. 48″. Maroon coloured foilage.

Rudbeckia (cone flower) HHA. Daisy type flower with cone centre. Yellow and Autumn colours.

Salvia horminum HA. 18″. 'Monarch Bouquet' gives several colours.

Verbascum bombyciferum B. 5′. Good grey leaves.

Dianthus barbatus *(sweet William) a useful biennial*

Glossary

An abstract flower arrangement. A design which is not naturalistic and is the opposite of landscape.

Accessories. Objects other than plant material and used in or with flower arrangements such as candles, figurines and plates.

Annual. A plant which grows from seed to maturity in one year and then dies.

Base. A stand or flat piece of stone, wood, metal or fabric on which an arrangement may be placed.

Bedding Plant. A plant used for temporary display in a flower bed, often in quantity. It is usually grown almost to flowering stage elsewhere.

Biennial. A plant which takes two seasons to grow from seed to maturity and then dies.

Boiling water treatment. Flowers which wilt in an arrangement may be revived by cutting off an inch of stem and then placing the stem end in an inch of boiling water. This removes part of any air bubble and the hot water travels quickly up the stem. Some flower arrangers advocate doing this to cut plant material at the time of preparation especially to flowers which have difficulty in taking up water. The flower should be protected with paper but the stem may be left in the water until it cools.

Bonemeal. A fertiliser made from ground bones which has little immediate effect on growth but gives a steady slow action over a long period and helps the formation of roots. It can be applied in Autumn and Winter and is normally used at a rate of 2–4 oz. per sq. yd. (or one good handful).

Budded. Ingrafted into alien stock.

Bulb. A modified bud usually formed under the ground. It stores food during a resting period in fleshy scales or swollen leaf bases and contains a shoot or complete embryo flower in the centre.

Callus. A growth of corky tissue which forms naturally over any wound in a plant. It can prevent water from entering a cut stem end.

Catkin. A particular kind of flower spike which is often pendulous and without petals, surrounded with scale-like bracts. A willow has erect catkins – 'pussy willow'.

Compost. Garden refuse which has rotted. This is accelerated by sprinkling a bought compost 'accelerator' over layers about 8″ thick. Wet, if the material is dry. When decayed apply to beds. Do not put diseased plants, seedy weeds or woody plant material on the compost heap. Compost also refers to a composition or mixture of such things as peat, manure, lime and so on.

Conditioning. A collective term used to cover any processes used which help to fill a cut stem with water.

Container. The term now used in place of 'vases' to refer to any receptacle which holds the stem ends of cut plant material.

Corm. A storage organ similar to a bulb but having no separate layers, e.g. gladioli, crocus.

Crown. Generally used to refer to the upper part of a rootstock from which shoots grow and to which they die back.

Cutting. A portion of leaf, stem or root separated from a plant and used in a flower arrangement or, in gardening, treated in such a way that it produces roots and eventually a new plant.

Deadheading. Removing dead flowers from a plant to encourage new growth.

Deciduous. The opposite to evergreen. Losing leaves annually and usually in winter.

Desiccant. A substance which can withdraw water from plant material and retain it. It is used for drying flowers. Examples are silica gel, borax, alum, sand. It must be dried in a warm oven after use.

Digging. Breaking up the ground up to a spade's depth and turning it right over to expose the lower soil to the beneficial influence of weather and to kill weeds. Put the soil from the first trench dug across a plot into a barrow and wheel it to the other end. Put the soil from the second trench into the first one and so on. The barrowload goes into the last trench. Manure or decayed garden refuse can be spread along the bottom of each trench.

Disbudding. The removal of some buds or shoots to concentrate the energies of the plant into a few buds which are developed to their fullest extent. Bigger flowers are the result of this.

Division. Cutting, pulling or teasing roots apart.

Dormant. Resting.

Double. This refers to flowers filled with petals as opposed to one in which the stamens and pistil can be seen.

Driftwood. Woody stems, branches, bark, root or chunks of wood which have been separated from the growing tree and weathered by the elements.

Drill. A narrow furrow made in soil usually for sowing seeds.

Drying. Removing water from plant material in order to keep it for a longer period. This can be done by air circulation, pressing under a weight or by burying it in a desiccant.

Everlasting. Applied to papery petalled flowers which last a long time and dry especially easily.

Feeding. Enriching soil to grow better plants. Compound fertilisers may be bought for general use and should be used according to instructions on the packet. Some gardens may need a special fertiliser and advice should be taken.

Flower arrangement. A general term for a composition of any plant material which may or may not contain flowers.

Foliage. Leaves of plants.

Forcing. Hurrying plants into growth by placing in gentle heat.

Germination. The earliest stage in the development of a seed; its sprouting.

Glaucous. Bluish grey.

Glycerine. A colourless, odourless solvent obtainable from chemists and used for preserving foliage.

Hardening-off. Gradual adjustment to lower temperatures. Blueing or yellowing of foliage or stoppage of growth means a plant has been exposed too rapidly.

Hardy. Capable of living over winter without artificial protection. It is relative to local climate.

Heeling in. Temporary planting when plants are dormant. Useful for Spring bulbs which are to be replaced by bedding out plants and have not finished growth.

Herbaceous. The opposite of woody or shrubby and usually applied to plants with top growth which dies down each year.

Hoeing. Breaking up the surface soil to kill weeds by disturbing weed seedlings and severing larger ones.

Humus. A brown or black material formed by the partial decomposition of vegetable or animal matter in or on the soil. It improves the texture of the soil and provides plant food.

Inorganic. Composed of matter other than vegetable or animal, in gardening it indicates a chemical fertiliser.

John Innes Compost. Not a trade name but a standardized formula for a mixture of sterilized loam, peat and sand which is sold ready made up for those who have no facilities for mixing their own. The various kinds are known by numbers. Seed compost for sowing seeds

No. 1 for cuttings and small plants

No. 2 for larger plants and bulbs

No. 3 for larger plants needing a richer diet.

Landscape style. A naturalistic flower arrangement copying a realistic scene.

Latex. Milky sap which leaks from flower stems such as poppy.

Line arrangement. A design with dominant lines and using little plant material.

Manure. Animal excreta.

Mass arrangement. A design using a lot of plant material and little space.

Mechanics. A collective term for devices which hold plant material in position.

Mulch. Any substance such as straw, peat, spread upon the ground to protect the roots of plants from heat, cold or drought.

Offset. Short side shoot from stem or root serving for propagation.

Organic. Derived from living things.

Peat. Partially decomposed plant material, especially mosses, which has little food value for plants but improves the texture of the soil.

Perennial. A plant whose life is at least three seasons.

A period arrangement. A design in the manner of a period in history, usually pre-Edwardian.

pH. A symbol for a scale which measures the degree of acidity or alkalinity of soil. Below pH 7 is acid and above is alkaline. Some plants dislike an alkaline (lime or chalk) soil.

Pinching (or stopping). Removing the growing tip of a plant in order to make it produce side growths.

Pinholder. A support for stem ends made by embedding pins in lead with the sharp end uppermost.

Plant material. Any part of a plant living or dried including leaves, flowers, fruit, stems, roots.

Plaque. A hanging design of plant material with a visible background.

Plastic foam. A water-retaining material for use in supplying cut plant material with water and holding stems in position.

Pot-et-fleur. Growing plants and cut flowers combined together.

Potting. Placing plants in pots, repotting is transferring from one pot to another – usually into a bigger one.

Preserving. To keep from decaying. In flower arrangement it refers to plants preserved with glycerine.

Pressed flower picture. A design of pressed plant material stuck on to a background, under glass in a picture frame.

Pricking out. Transplanting seedlings from the receptacle in which they have been raised to one with more room.

Pruning. To cut off or cut out superfluous parts or branches for good shaping, removing dead, damaged or diseased parts, to control quantity and quality of flowers and/or fruit.

Puddling. Filling the planting hole with water and letting it drain before putting in a plant.

Raking. Breaking up lumps of soil by pushing a rake forwards and backwards.

Retarding. Slowing growth of cut plant material usually by keeping colder or withholding water.

Shrub. A woody plant usually low-growing with several stems.

Staking. Supporting plants usually with a bamboo cane.

Stock. A plant to which a shoot or bud is joined and which provides the root system. Rose bushes are produced on stock.

Spit. A spade's depth of soil, usually 10".

Sucker. A growth direct from the stock, especially on roses, which must be removed or the plant reverts to a wild rose.

Swag. A hanging decoration of plant material without a visible background.

Tender. Not hardy and liable to injury from cold.

Tepid. Slightly warm, lukewarm.

Texture. The surface quality of material. In flower arrangement visual texture is more important than actual texture.

Thinning. Removing some plants in a group to give the remaining ones more room.

Traditional flower arrangement. A classical mass design often in a triangle, circle or oval.

Transpiration. The loss of water as a vapour from the exposed surfaces of plants.

Top dressing. Substance such as fertiliser or manure placed on the top of the soil and not worked in.

Tuber. A swollen, usually underground stem or root used for storage of food during resting times.

Turgid. Distended with water in the case of stems of plants. Stems which are not turgid are floppy.

Union. The place where a shoot or bud is joined to the stock.

Underplanting. Growing plants below taller plants.

Variegated. White, cream or yellow markings on foliage.

Wilting. Lacking in water content and drooping.

Where to Buy Plants

There are many excellent nurseries and garden centres throughout the British Isles. If you cannot find the plants you want to buy locally, then the following addresses should be useful.

General

Bees Ltd.
Sealand
Chester CH1 6BA

Hillier and Sons
Winchester

Scott's Royal Nurseries
Merriott, Somerset

Sunningdale Nurseries Ltd.
Windlesham, Surrey

R. C. Notcutt Ltd.
Woodbridge
Suffolk

Bulbs

Daffodils

M. J. Jefferson-Brown
Whitbourne, Worcester

Irises and Alliums

Orpington Nurseries Co. Ltd.
Rocky Lane, Gatton Park
Reigate, Surrey RH2 0TA

Tulips

Walter Blom and Son Ltd.
Coombelands Nurseries
Leavesden, Watford, Herts

Perennials

Bressingham Gardens
Diss, Norfolk IP22 2AB

R. Poland
Brook House Nursery
Highbrook Road
Ardingly, Sussex

Eldon Nurseries
Corfe Mullein
Wimborne, Dorset

Delphiniums

Blackmore and Langdon
Twerton Hill Nursery
Bath, Somerset

Cottage Garden Flowers

The Margory Fish Nursery
East Lambrook Manor
South Petherton, Somerset

Unusual Plants

The Plantsmen
Buckshaw Gardens
Holwell, Sherborne, Dorset

Peonies and Irises

Kelway and Son Ltd.
Langport, Somerset

165

Grey-leafed Plants

Mrs Desmond Underwood
Ramparts Nurseries
Colchester, Essex CO4 5BD

Roses

Flower Arrangers' Roses

E. B. Le Grice (Roses) Ltd.
North Walsham, Norfolk

Miniature Roses

C. Gregory and Son Ltd.
The Rose Garden, Stapleford
Nottingham NG9 7JA

Old Roses

Edwin Murrell Nurseries
Shrewsbury

Seeds

Carters Tested Seeds Ltd.
Raynes Park, London SW20

Suttons Seeds Ltd.
London Road, Reading, Berks

Thompson and Morgan Ltd.
Ipswich, Suffolk

W. J. Unwin Ltd., Seedsmen
Histon, Cambridge

NOTE: *These addresses have been selected by Jean Taylor and their inclusion here does not imply recommendation or endorsement by Thames Television.*

Learning More

The location of Flower Arrangement Clubs for flower arrangement demonstrations, shows and practice meetings can be found by contacting The National Association of Flower Arrangement Societies of Great Britain
21a Denbigh Street, London SW1
Telephone 01 828 5145

Information about classes in flower arrangement and horticulture may be obtained from your local Education Officer or from a College of Further Education.

Useful Addresses

The Royal Horticultural Society
Vincent Square, London SW1P 2PE

Membership (called Fellowship) is open to *anyone* interested and benefits include a monthly Journal, gardening advice, library privileges, free attendance at Shows, including Chelsea, and admission to the Society's Garden at Wisley in Surrey.

The Royal National Rose Society
Bone Hill, Chiswell Green Lane
St Albans, Herts.

Membership is open to *anyone* interested and benefits include the Society's Journal and admission to the gardens at the above address.

'Gardens of England and Wales Open to the Public'

20p from booksellers or 28p from
The National Gardens Scheme
57 Lower Belgrave Street, London WS1 0LR

'Gardens to Visit'

10p from W. H. Smith or 13p from
The Gardeners' Sunday Organization
The Organizer, White Witches, Claygate Road
Dorking, Surrey

'Scotland's Gardens'

25p from
The Organizer
Scotland's Gardens Scheme
26 Castle Terrace, Edinburgh EH1 2EL

'Historic Houses, Castles and Gardens in Great Britain and Northern Ireland'

30p from bookstalls or 42p from
ABC Travel Guides Ltd.
Oldhill, London Road, Dunstable LU6 3EB

'The National Trust Guide to Properties Open'

13p from
The National Trust
42 Queen Anne's Gate, London SW1

*Floradesac Ltd., Cedar Lodge, Allington, Chippenham, Wiltshire.
For Flora-D-Hydrate (silica gel with a grain suitable for drying flowers).*